SHOPPING FOR FURNITURE

A SELECTION OF QUOTES FROM FANS AND REVIEWS OF THE FIRST EDITION OF *SHOPPING FOR FURNITURE: A CONSUMER'S GUIDE*

"A "must have" no nonsense title. Mr. Lewin has the right idea: inform the public about how to make better choices, and you have a reader who will pass on the word."

— Andrea from Arkansas.

"The book was indispensable in helping me deal with retailers by giving me the confidence and power to sift through superfluous information and get to the essential facts. Mr. Lewin was even so kind as to return my phone call to answer a question I had about a certain manufacturer."

— Patrick from Pennsylvania

"The Best Furniture Shopping Education You Can Get! This book is great! It tells new consumers what to look for and what they are paying for. The illustrations are great and the terminology is easy to understand. Mr. Lewin does not suggest that you buy only top of the line furniture; he urges you to consider the purpose and the abuse/use a piece of furniture will take. Furniture shopping to me is like looking in a museum. Although I knew a lot, I still found things to highlight in his book. I plan on buying this book for Christmas, wedding and graduation gifts."

— Jelane from Texas.

"Hi, Mr. Lewin. I wanted to say that your book was great! It was a book I needed to read last year when I was struggling with how to begin the furniture shopping process. I'm glad I found the book. It has answered a lot of my questions on furniture."

— Laura

"Shopping for Furniture teaches anyone how to tell a real sales price from an everyday price, which manufactures are best, the pros and cons of buying through an 800 number, and how to find the best furniture stores. Len Lewin shows how to choose the furniture you need at the best price you can get. Recommended."

— James A. Cox, The Midwest Book Review.

"Armed with this book, it's easy to furnish your home with confidence. Lewin trains the reader to recognize good design, construction, value and more."

— Jim Carlson, Country Almanac magazine

SHOPPING FOR FURNITURE

A CONSUMER'S GUIDE

Second Edition

By
Leonard Bruce Lewin

Linden Publishing, Inc.
Fresno

SHOPPING FOR FURNITURE: A CONSUMER'S GUIDE
Second Edition

by
Leonard Bruce Lewin

Text © 2004 by Leonard Bruce Lewin
Illustrations © 2004 Linden Publishing
Illustrations by James Goold
Veneer photographs pages 16-17 by Patternwork Veneering, Inc.,
Bill Hull, President

123456789
ISBN 0-941936-87-2

PRINTED IN SINGAPORE

Library of Congress Cataloging-in-Publication Data

Lewin, Leonard Bruce, 1937-
      Shopping for furniture : a consumer's guide / by Leonard Bruce Lewin.— 2nd ed.
         p. cm.
      Includes index.
      ISBN 0-941936-87-2 (pbk. : alk. paper)
      1. Furniture—Purchasing. I. Title.
      TS885.L45 2004
      645'.4'029—dc22   2004002034

LINDEN
PUBLISHING

2006 S. Mary, Fresno, Ca 93721
800-345-4447 • www.lindenpub.com

This book is dedicated to Elaine Weir Lewin: my wife, my best friend, my soulmate, the love of my life. Thank you, Peanut.

CONTENTS

ACKNOWLEDGEMENTS . . . . **ix**

INTRODUCTION . . . . **xi**

1 HISTORY **1**
Furniture from Cleopatra to Napoleon to Us!

2 WOOD AND VENEER **11**
How to Spot Quality in Tables and Casegoods

3 WOOD FINISHING **33**
The Coating Protects and Beautifies the Furniture

4 SHOPPING FOR WOOD **40**
Never Pay Full Retail! Never!

5 UPHOLSTERY **62**
Color and Comfort on Display; But Quality Is Hidden Underneath!

6 BUYING UPHOLSTERY **70**
Choosing the Right Fabric Is the Most Expensive Decision

7 LEATHER **86**
Its Rich Beauty Comes from Natural Variations!

8   PERSONAL STYLE **93**
Of Recliners and Designers, and How to Get the Best from Each

9   THE STORE IS NOT THE ENEMY! **98**
Preparation Is the Key

10   BRANDS AND STORES **101**
Here's Where to Shop for Furniture, Wherever You Live

11   ADVERTISING **123**
Reading Between the Lines Helps You Become a Smarter Shopper!

12   LEARNING MORE ABOUT IT ALL! **130**
You Already Know How to Shop!

TO THE READER **134**

INDEX **135**

ACKNOWLEDGEMENTS

As I look back over my thirty-six years in the furniture industry, I can think of so many people who have influenced me, cared for me, molded me, stretched me, given me fits, and given me joy. I want not only to thank them, but also to applaud them. It is such a joy when a vocation becomes an avocation, when a job becomes an adventure, when that adventure becomes a journey, and when that journey becomes an identity. With great appreciation, I would like to present my fellow travelers, who showed me the way:

Elliott Wood, who gave me my start. Fred Councill, who always had time for a young man. George Ayars, the salesman who was with me in the beginning. Cliff Wright, who gave me my first order: He didn't need it, but he knew I did. Howard Haworth, a leader who always inspired. Meta Best, my "business mother". Earl Ladlow, who showed me what "balance" is. Helen Fransis, who cared, and who taught me what upholstery was all about. Charlie Wilson, a friend, a boss, a gentleman. Eddie Mathews, my pal. Mike Elliott, who made the business fun. Bob Meloskie, who taught me more than I ever needed to know. Denny Doud, the best storyteller the planet has ever known. Those two sweet angels, Sarah and Lovie, who brought to the simplest of tasks a dignity and joy that always inspired and warmed me. Caroline Baker, my Gal Friday, who kept me out of trouble every day of the week. The Schatz family in Oregon and the Ennis family in Idaho and Washington, who each represent the best of what a local furniture dealer can give to a community and to the industry. The Flegel family in Menlo Park, California;

the Slater family in Fresno and Modesto; the Swartz family in San Rafael, California, and the Sorsky family in Fresno—the wives, the sons, the fathers, the daughters, who gave me and gave their customers warmth, integrity and knowledge, and who made "service" a commitment to excellence, not just a word in a business journal. Al Firenzi, a son who took a father's small store and made it big, and who stayed the course better than anyone else. Vince Palumbo, a pal, and a buyer who made it fun. Frank Blauvelt, a true mentor and a lovely, caring man who taught me so much. Frank Scofield, my "business father", who trusted me and gave me the chance to learn the business at his side, even though he was always telling me to get lost.

All these people and more have made me a "rich" man, but there is one more who filled me with joy and laughter, who shared not only the business with me, but who also shared himself. It is rare in this world to experience the wonder of a total friend who was and is always there for me—my buddy, Stan Lush.

Thank you, all. I must also thank Barbara Gallo, a friend, an author, and a computer maven, without whose technical help and ever-availability this book could not have been written.

Leonard B. Lewin
March 12, 1998
Fair Oaks, California

As you can see, I wrote this acknowledgement in March of 1998, and here I am with the 2nd Edition of my book and I wouldn't change a word. I should say though that the reception the 1st Edition of my book has had with consumers from all over the nation has been wonderfully warm and very supportive. For this I want to say thank you and to you new consumers I want to say welcome to the world of furniture.

Leonard B. Lewin
January 3, 2004
Folsom, California

INTRODUCTION

I have learned quite a lot about what furniture consumers are interested in over the past five years, since the First Edition of my book was published. The countless e-mails and phone calls asking for advice have all reinforced my original contention that most consumers simply do not have a clue about how to be smart furniture shoppers. It is not their fault, and it is not your fault. The furniture industry, both the retailers and the manufacturers, still have not come to grips with how to educate consumers about what is so special about furniture and why it is so complicated a consideration. I expect that by the time I get to the 5th Edition nothing will have changed. Let's begin to make you a smart furniture shopper. Life's too short to wait for help from the industry.

To begin with, I'll tell you what you will not get out of this book:

1. You will not become an authority on the history of furniture.
2. You will not become an interior designer.
3. You will not know how to upholster furniture.
4. You will not, absolutely not, become an expert on anything except how to shop for furniture, and how to stop wasting money on the wrong purchase.

I hope you will come to know furniture as something more than a commodity and begin to view it as a wonderfully complex, changing, fascinating world of art and utility; shape and form; color and texture; treasures and finds; heirlooms and even things for Goodwill. I want you to enjoy the fascinating world of furniture in which I have worked for so many years. I want to share my discoveries and help make buying furniture a more enjoyable experience for you.

With this in mind, don't expect too much, but then again, don't miss my point: the world of furniture is more than just discounts and missed golf dates. Truly take the time to make your home a refuge from this mad world and you will find that your home will regenerate you and send you out each morning with a feeling of warmth and security. On your return, it will be a haven that makes the busiest of days easier to take.

"Twenty per cent off, forty per cent off, no payments, no interest!" No! No! No! Sadly, this is how our exposure to the world of furniture often begins today. In all fairness, with adjustments for each era's own style of merchandising, this may have always been the case.

Looking back at any activity or at any items over a span of many years, we are often overly critical of the current era. Our view of the past is always filtered through present-day attitudes, and a real look is often impossible. But even with this in mind, my reason for writing this book is to try to tempt you to look at furniture in a new light. This category of consumer goods is more than just discounts. It is a continuing thread, a link to our past, and a haven for the present. I want you to see it for what it has always really been: a collection of items that make our space, our home, more comfortable and more inviting; that make it a true retreat from the mad pace and cares of the day; that make it a place to be safe, a place to be comfortable, a place to be enjoyed.

One of the great problems in modern society is the disconnectedness of the individual from the system to which he or she is, ironically, connected. While it is true that "no man is an island," it is also true that "Everyman" today is increasingly removed from others in everyday activities. We are, more and more, merely small parts of an increasingly large community of business and industrial systems, in which the individual plays an ever-diminished role as a part of a larger whole. So we are often buying meat from Australia, clothes from China, cars from Germany, and furniture from the Philippines, and living in an increasingly anonymous world where the producers of these products are unknown to us.

Gone are the days when we ate eggs from a neighbor's farm, or dined on a table constructed from the maple or cherry trees in the forest or orchard around the bend. We no longer use items made by the craftsman who sat beside us in church or in the pub. Gone are the personal connections with the everyday things in our lives, the connections that gave these things a personality and a reality beyond the simple fact that they exist. Of course, along with these romantic musings, the great scourges of the past are gone also, and for that we can be thankful.

I am not suggesting we should view the past with romantic nostalgia. The past had but a limited number of affluent people and certainly very few enjoyed the good life. The current large middle class, despite all its problems, still represents one of the great advances in man's history on this planet. In the midst of this growing material prosperity and decreased personal appreciation of the objects that surround us, I want to reconnect you with the melody that resonates from our furniture whenever we take time to listen to its song in our day-to-day lives. Did I say that? Don't panic. I am going to show you how to have it all—not only the song, but also the discounts and values. Impossible? Only when you don't know the notes.

Before we begin, I want to give you a brief list of terms and expressions furniture professionals use. I will often use them, as a matter of course, not to confuse you but simply because they have become part of my vocabulary. When I am in my furniture mode, I forget that we are not all old salesmen.

Upper-end: A term used to describe the more expensive product, store, or manufacturer.

Lower-end: This is the opposite of upper-end, thus describing the less expensive product, store or manufacturer.

Casegoods: Describes any wood furniture that is essentially composed of a "case": Large chests, dressers, china cabinets, armoires, night stands, but the term can also include any items closely associated with the cases, like dining chairs, headboards and mirrors.

Occasional: Usually describes all smaller wood furniture found in the living room, den or any other area: Cocktail tables, end tables, accessory tables, curio cabinets, mirrors not specifically made to match a collection.

Collection: A term used by the manufacturer to describe a group of furniture with a common design theme. For example, the Drexel-Heritage Heirlooms Collection is made up of wonderful eighteenth-century-style mahogany pieces: all items in this collection will have a common theme and be tied together by the finish.

Suite: A term used to describe a group of bedroom or dining room furniture within a collection. Pronounced "suit" as in suit of clothes.

Hand: A term that describes the feel of a piece of upholstery fabric or leather. If an item has a wonderful "hand" it feels good to the touch. This word is seldom used for anything but fabric or leather.

Accessory Items: A wide range of items that go into a room: Pictures, table-top items, dry plants and flowers, metal objects—almost anything, other than furniture, used to decorate a room.

Table-Top Items: This term is really self-descriptive, referring to objects that normally sit on top of a cocktail table, end table, or even a dining table.

Deck: This term refers to the area under the cushions on a sofa or chair. You may hear someone say that it is an eight-way hand-tied deck, etc. It is simply the area that everything rests on, yourself included.

Deep Finish: Refers to the best of finishes, in which many finish steps and many "layers" of finish material result in a richness that seems to have great depth and clarity. This is hard to describe, but easy to recognize, even if you don't know the term.

Most of these terms came into the furniture vocabulary as producers communicated with the retail trade, and from within the manufacturing organization itself, as short-cuts to define what is being done. Over the years, the words have moved out of the specific and into the vocabulary of retail designers and salespeople—not to mention the occasional writer. Now let's start by taking a brief look at the history of the furniture items in our lives.

1

....

HISTORY
Furniture from Cleopatra to Napoleon to Us!

The time of Egypt's New Kingdom, about 1300 BC, is where the known story of the furniture objects in our lives begins. Egyptian artisans gave us the armchair, for instance. It was in Egypt that wood turnings were first used to create interesting shapes for table and chair legs. In an effort to demonstrate power over their environment, Egyptians often carved the ends of their chair legs and table legs with hooves of cattle, talons of great hawks, or paws of lions. Inlays of gold, silver and precious gems were used on the more important pieces made for temples, tombs or palaces.

Egyptians were the first craftsmen to experiment with using thin layers of exotic woods over less expensive woods to create veneer panels, and they probably were the first merchants to answer the question: "Is veneered furniture as good as solid furniture?" Unfortunately, the first answer, "Yes", wasn't believed, and to this day there is still lively debate on the subject. (By the way, the answer still is "Yes".)

With the rise of the Greek civilization around 400 BC, and with the belief that "truth" or the "essential nature" of the universe was revealed by nature's laws, it isn't surprising that the Greeks brought to furniture a fine sense of mathematical proportion. Low beds, similar to our daybeds, were often used, along with many pillows and low tables. Altar tables and chests for the storage of valuables could be found in temples and in the homes of the wealthy.

But it was the Romans, with their far-reaching conquests and stable government, who created the first semblance of a leisure class. They borrowed from the

Greeks and Egyptians the best of their cultures, including their furniture designs. This leisure class gave rise to a need for furniture that went beyond the purely utilitarian.

These three great civilizations, spanning a few thousand years, were marked by relatively stable governments which produced structured societies and allowed development of an infrastructure that encouraged the minor arts. But the disintegration of the Roman Empire and the dawn of the Early Middle Ages—with sweeping tides of social change riding on the horses of death, pestilence, war, and famine—plunged the world into a seven hundred-year night wherein little cultural advancement came about. Strife, unrest, and grinding poverty for the population as a whole, provided little opportunity or incentive for development of items to meet the less essential needs of society. During these times, the only significant furniture items produced were for the church or the nobility. These large, heavy oak pieces, collectively known as the Romanesque Style, were of limited everyday use but we can still see their shapes in our churches today.

When the Normans invaded England in 1066 AD, the Saxon defenders were still living in crude huts with little more than a chest to qualify as furniture. These invaders, needing to secure their military bases and control the countryside, built stone castles around which villages and towns grew. Then, around these towns, cities began to grow.

The military necessity for secure bases, and the growing political influence of the church (Christian in the West and Muslim in the East) combined and gave impetus to the rise of population centers with all the support structure that is still common today—farms to supply food, shipping centers to move goods, artisans to produce tools and items of commerce—all supplying the needs of an increasing concentration of people in specific locations.

With this concentration of people came a wider distribution of wealth, but the church and nobility still controlled the greater share and thus were the primary users of most furniture items of this period—large trestle tables and big hutches or chests, usually done in oak. Decorated with linen-fold carvings, this look can still be seen in stores today. Benches, stools, iron stands for torches, candles, wall hangings to keep the chill off those early stone buildings—all remain a part of our homes as drapes, table decor, and dining room furniture.

But with the dawning of the Renaissance Period there began a refinement of furniture items into shapes and categories that are a large part of today's furniture scene. Upholstered items date from this period. Lighter, more graceful designs of wood furniture began to appear. The development of the idea of private property, an alien concept until then, and the rise of a merchant class with smaller homes and more clearly defined political rights, made the family unit a growing economic factor. A great sweep of new ideas, trade and exploration brought newer ideas, newer goods, newer expectations and newer desires to people in all parts of Europe and

---

WHAT'S AN ANTIQUE?

By one popular definition, an item of furniture must be over 100 years old to be considered an antique.

By another definition, it must have been made before 1820, the approximate start of the Industrial Revolution.

In either case, just being old doesn't make it valuable, though it sure does help.

Asia. The Italian workman was sought after as the *primo* interpreter of this age, and his skills inspired and influenced all regional furniture design.

Comfort and elegance, as well as function, became the driving forces behind furniture of this era. Oak was still the primary wood used, and carving the primary decorative motif. The Tudor rose, Tudor arch, Roman acanthus leaf, floral carvings, even the downward slope of a chair arm—all sprang from this era, and all can still be found in your local stores.

As was the case from the beginning, furniture design was very much influenced by political and social factors of the time. Narrow tables with a bench on one side were not so much a design statement as a reflection of a host's need to sit with his back to a wall in order to feel secure from enemies or roving bandits. So much for the designer!

Each locale—England, France, Holland, Italy, Spain, the cities of the Far East— contributed regional twists to the furniture produced by their craftsmen. The great tides of political change had a subtle but powerful influence on how furniture was designed in all these periods. The Moorish influence in Spain, Cromwell and the Puritans in England, exiled monarchs returning to England after being influenced by the French court, merchant kings—all the tides of social unrest had an effect on designs in each society.

Walnut came to the fore during Queen Anne's reign. Armless chairs were needed to accommodate women in billowing gowns. Chests became necessary for displaying the new china items. Even the gentlemen dandies of the day needed room in which to lay the long tails of their coats when seated in a chair. The real, perhaps unimportant, needs of society were dictating the shapes and styles of furniture.

Small desks, graceful mirrors, dressing tables, great canopied beds, all sprang from the French court of Louis XIV in particular. The full flowering of the court during this time saw a high point (or low point, in some opinions) of intricate and extensive decoration, curves, shapes of all description, detail upon detail—really a degree of design hubris that reflected the same arrogance found in the attitudes of the aristocracy. Walnut, mahogany, satinwood, rosewood, tulip wood, all found their way into the furniture of this period of great luxury for the few: Breakfast tables, even tables for chocolates, small specific-function items that gave rise to the excessiveness of this most opulent court.

Paralleling this period of the French courts of Louis XIV, XV and XVI was, in England, the period of the Georges: I, II, III and IV. From 1714 to 1820 was a time of many new interpretations in furniture design. Driven by the great designers, Chippendale, Adams, Hepplewhite, and Sheraton, and fueled by economic success, this era of change saw the rise of a significantly large class of wealthy landowners and merchants ranking below the nobility, who desired and could afford fine furniture items. This new concentration of wealth, which had

THE TRUTH ABOUT MAHOGANY!

For two hundred and fifty years, mahogany was the most sought-after cabinet wood in the world. There are three types of this wood, *Khaya ivorensis* (African mahogany), *Swietenia macrophylla* (Honduras mahogany), and *Shorea* (Philippine mahogany), of which only one is true mahogany. All three are used in furniture today. Only the Honduras variety is a true mahogany. It is used in fine furniture, as is African mahogany. Philippine mahogany is considered an inferior substitute.

Mahogany was the wood of choice for delicate and graceful shapes, for furniture that was not only more sensibly scaled for smaller rooms, but that also reflected the growing sense of security and individual personality characterizing the age.

been growing since Renaissance times, coupled with new labor-saving tools and mechanical devices, made possible the production of more furniture at better prices than ever before.

And then, in the late eighteenth century, came Napoleon.

Initially there was a reaction against the excesses of the collective Kings Louis. The Directoire Period of Napoleon, as this time is known in the furniture industry, exhibited less elaborate shapes, and cleaner lines. It was almost a Spartan statement, with a campaign theme reflecting the Ultimate Soldier's needs; but this, with Bonaparte's growing sense of Empire and megalomania, quickly changed. The Napoleonic "N" and his favorite bumblebee motif carried the furniture of this period to as many excesses as the period of any of the Louis.

At the end of the eighteenth century, the United States was still, in matters of furniture, a British colony. There were, of course, a handful of innovative designers—Goddard, Randolph, Savery, and Duncan Phyfe—but the furniture of early America was, for the most part, a derivative of English and French designs. When these designs were carried out in the woods of the American forests, however, a whole new feeling resulted. Warmer, more casual, often smaller-scaled, these pieces were adaptations on continental themes, but different—and wonderfully so. America did produce its own version of the Victorian style that came out of England and, in many respects, was truly representative of the Manifest Destiny mood of the American people of that age: Large, over-scaled, sometimes ugly (Duncan Phyfe thought so) but, at the very least, expansive in its intent and expression

For me, one of the great curiosities of our furniture world today is the fact that the vast majority of styles selling today were designed in the seventeenth, eighteenth, and nineteenth centuries. Despite all of our technological advancements, we still turn to these early designs for the look we want in our homes. Furniture stores still feature collection after collection of eighteenth century furniture. In today's furniture world the buzz words are not so much Georgian, Jacobean, Directoire or Empire, but rather formal and informal or casual. Whatever the term used, the shape and feel are definitely yesterday's.

THE SETTEE.

Do you know that the "Settee" replaced the "Settle" in the 17th Century? It seems the "Settle" was just too uncomfortable and thus the "Settee" came into being as a sitting area for more than one person. At the beginning a wooden, bench-like item with a spindle back, the "Settee" was the pre-cursor to today's sofas!

IS THERE A THEORY OF DESIGN?

The better question for us as consumers would be is there a design secret that we should keep in mind when we are looking at furniture items in a store? Is there some secret of proportion and style that makes one design better than another? Remember I promised you in the first pages of the book that you would not become an expert in furniture design after you read this book. I just mentioned to you that I am amazed that today's consumer is still buying yesterday's designs for their homes! How can this be? Well it defies logic at the very least. Think about this fact: the only furniture items that are new to us today would be the computer desk and the entertainment center, and these are intended to give us a place for all our

The busy bee was Napoleon's emblem and is still common on many fabrics, usually chair fabrics, found in upper-end furniture stores.

computer and entertainment equipment! Think about that! Two new items when it comes to furniture and here we are in 2004!

Every other item that we use in our home is an item that first saw the light of day many, many years ago. Oh, we have recliners today and Louie 14th didn't have this luxury, and we may have better mattresses today than Henry the 8th had, but these advances are mere variations on the basic theme. So what does all this mean when it comes to a theory of design. There are countless theories and countless rules as to what determines good design but let me let you in on a secret: each and everyone of us can tell a good design from a bad design, even though we may not be able to verbalize why one design is better than another. Another factor to keep in mind is that whatever appeals to you is for you a good design. Who cares if your Aunt Helen thinks your dining room is ugly (unless, of course, you are in Aunt Helen's will). Don't confuse your search for the perfect furniture items for your home with considerations of whether or not French Country items are "better" than formal 18th Century English items. Your eye and your lifestyle will determine what is best for you. Go with your gut. You know what you like. Go with that and let the arguments about design elements be something interior designers talk about on their lunch hour.

Questions you will be asked by a designer or salesperson include: "What is your lifestyle? How do you like your home to look? Do you put your feet up on the coffee table? Do you entertain a lot?" And, depending on your answers, you will be shown either the best of the eighteenth century or a variation of its country cousin. For the relative few who like a "modern" look the usual answer to the question, "Where can I find real modern furniture?" is apt to be: "I'm not sure who carries it." You may have to travel to a large metropolitan market area in order to find any significant amount of modern furniture on display.

Thus the history of furniture design developed until the eighteenth and nineteenth centuries and, in many respects, stayed there. Contemporary furniture, or the more extreme category called modern, has had limited appeal and this, in itself, is a fascinating area for study. If furniture has been a reflection of the age and society that produced it, and I believe that to be the case, why hasn't the twentieth and now the twenty-first century produced a style capturing the imagination of consumers? It is true that a number of secondary styles did develop, such as Arts and Crafts, Art Nouveau, Shaker and others; however, the broad categories of furniture styles have not changed much since the nineteenth century.

The answer may be no more complicated than the basic question the industry asks itself and the customer: "Are you formal or informal?" As a response to this question, manufacturers produce the furniture you see in stores. We simply do not have a "style identity" that is uniquely our century's.

One other fact must be kept in mind: In the age that produced what we now call formal furniture, there was no such question. The lifestyle of the nobility was

THE SOFA.

Did you know that the upholstered sofa that we know and love today didn't emerge until around 1830 when deep-buttoned, coil-spring upholstery became available?

formal. Country folk, and anyone else far removed from the court, simply produced or purchased rough copies of everything done at court. The copied items were done in local woods and finished in locally-available materials. It was that simple. Today, with wealth cutting across all manner of diverse lifestyles, there is no focal point at which to direct *any* effort, let alone the design of furniture (which ranks just below the development of sprinkler heads as a matter of national concern).

THEY DON'T MAKE FURNITURE LIKE THEY USED TO!

Is it true that they don't make furniture like they used to; or is it a common myth held by every generation? Frankly, at other times it might have been true, but it most definitely is not true now. Even today's modest furniture is far better than yesterday's routine furniture. Decent furniture, nicely styled, is currently available at very modest prices, and the best of present-day furniture is technically as good as any furniture ever produced. Now the key word is "technically". It goes without saying—even though I'll say it—that the craftsman of old, personally selecting the woods, preparing the glues, cutting each piece of wood to exacting proportions, working with hand tools and spending hundreds of hours on an item, often created true works of art. But the fact remains that carpentry, joinery, and cabinetmaking were slow, backbreaking kinds of work two hundred years ago. Today's commercial woodworker is aided by machines and techniques that can duplicate the work of yesterday's finest craftsmen. It wasn't even until the late nineteenth century that good sharpening stones were available to the cabinetmaker so he could keep a keen edge on his tools without spending an inordinate amount of time on the sharpening process.

> **OH THOSE GOTHS!**
> The style called "Gothic," which many people today consider the height of antique elegance, originally was a term of scornful disdain. Early examples of the style, when viewed by Italian artists and builders, were thought to be so bad that only a Goth could have made them. The Goths, you will recall, were the fifth century barbarians who destroyed Rome. Clearly the Italians were still upset about it.

Perhaps sadly (for those who love antiques) but truly, the combined efforts of today's team of designers and technicians, coupled with the most sophisticated computer-controlled machines, produces fine furniture to equal that of any age.

A Louis XVI mahogany writing table that President Kennedy used when signing a treaty or two sold for $1,400,000 in 1996. *USA Today* featured an article about Sotheby's auction of the possessions of the late Duke and Duchess of Windsor. The writing table where Edward VIII sat in 1936, to sign the document by which he abdicated the throne of England to become the Duke of Windsor, sold for $415,000. Two George II chairs sold for $34,500. Today, Baker, Henredon, Century, Stickley, Drexel-Heritage or Thomasville can—and do—produce these same styles of writing tables for between $1,800 and $3,000. They all make similar chairs for under $1,500. Now you say: "You are not comparing apples to apples! Furniture used by the Windsors or Kennedy are in a class apart." That is true from the historical viewpoint—and from the historical perspective the items were probably good buys—but strictly from a furniture standpoint, item to item, you can do a lot better buying from your local merchant.

It is very important, when looking at prices of antiques, to recognize that the vast price difference between antique and new items is due to the simple fact that relatively few antiques exist. If the historically-important antique can be authenticated as to the designer and craftsman who made it, the price will rise accordingly. Enormous price differences do **not** indicate technical woodworking qualities no longer in existence. The same techniques and materials are still with us. The big difference—without belaboring any artistic elements involved—is that a current day's production, by the best manufacturers of fine furniture, could well equal a year or two years of work for Chippendale or Hepplewhite. Our glues are better; wood is kiln-dried; finishes are better; joinery techniques are the same, if not better—and the design can certainly be as good. Granted, a new item may not have the soul of yesterday's fine table, but the "soul" for which we now spend a fortune has been determined by the fickle nature of history. Enjoy today's product. Be proud of it. Take care of it, and tomorrow you or your children may find it is a treasure.

FURNITURE DESIGN TIME-LINE

With this brief view backward to the roots of our furniture world in mind, let's now take a look at the elements that go into wood and upholstered furniture available in stores today. I will tell you how wood and upholstery furniture are made and finished, and tell you what to look for in order to make sure you get the greatest value for your dollar. But before we leave this section on history I want to give you a brief "Time-Line" for the key design elements that make up the history of furniture. This Time-Line was developed by John Pile in his very fine book "Interior Design", Harry N. Adams, Inc. New York in 1988. From the Egyptians to the Post-Modern period in 1966, the table on the facing page provides a sketch of what the furniture periods look like.

DESIGN STYLES IN FURNITURE STORES TODAY

Well, you are not going to find Egyptian, or Greek, or Roman. Rarely will you find Biedermeire, or Gothic, or Early Christian, or Byzantine. You certainly won't find De Stijl, and even if you find it you won't recognize it. I wouldn't. So why do we have this elaborate Time-Line? First, to impress my wife. Second, my publisher insisted on it. Third, I wanted you to know I have done my homework. But most importantly, I wanted to give you a sense of the history behind the furniture items you see in stores today. While you will rarely see any authentic design reproductions of our earliest furniture styles, you will constantly be seeing furniture items that have elements of all these styles incorporated in today's furniture designs.

For me, and I think for many of you, part of the joy of owning wonderful furniture items is to have a sense of their history. Their pedigree, so to speak. You will be seeing rather faithful "reproductions" at all price levels of some of our early styles: Chippendale, Sheraton, Queen Anne, Victorian, Colonial American, Arts and Crafts, Art Nouveau, and Modern; but more often than not in today's stores you

TIMELINE OF FURNITURE PERIODS

Egypt 3100-311 B.C.

Greece 650-30 B.C.

Rome 753 B.C. - A.D. 365

The Middle Ages

    Early Christian 300-500 A.D.

    Byzantine 323-1453

    Romanesque 800-1150

    Gothic 1150-1500

Italian Renaissance

    Early 1400-1500

    High 1500-1600

    Baroque 1600-1700

Spanish Renaissance 1400-1600

French Renaissance and Later Periods 1485-1643

    Louis XIV (Baroque) 1643-1700

    Regency 1700-1730

    Louis XV (Rococo) 1730-1760

    Louis XVI (Rococo/Neoclassic) 1760-1789

    Directoire 1795-1804

    Empire 1804-1815

German Biedermeier 1815-1848

English Renaissance and Later Periods

    Tudor 1485-1558

    Elizabethan 1558-1603

    Jacobean 1603-1649

Commonwealth 1649-1660

Restoration 1660-1702

Caroline 1660-1689

William and Mary 1689-1702

Queen Anne 1702-1714

Early Georgian 1714-1750

Middle Georgian (Chippendale) 1750-1770

Late Georgian 1770-1811

    (Adam 1728-1792)

    (Hepplewhite d. 1786)

    (Sheraton 1751-1806)

Regency 1811-1830

Victorian 1830-1901

American Early Colonial 1608-1720

    Georgian 1720-1789

    Federal 1789-1830

    Greek Revival 1815-1840

    Victorian 1830-1901

Arts and Crafts 1851-1914

Art Nouveau 1892-1905

De Stijl 1917-1929

Bauhaus 1919-1933

Art Deco 1918-1939

Modernism 1925-

Post Modernism 1966-

will be seeing eclectic (big buzz word today that you will hear tossed about by store designers and sales people: it means "a combination of many styles rolled into a package"), and you will be seeing combinations of many styles loosely grouped as a "Collection". You will see "Designer Collections" from the likes of Jill Ireland,

Martha Stewart, or Tommy Bahama and "Celebrity Collections" like The Hemmingway Collection or the Bogart Collection—and then there will be "Regional Collections" like Tuscany, or Sienna, perhaps Chambray, or Nottingham. These collections will be loosely "tied together" by their finish and will be wonderfully presented by clever and imaginative marketing programs. None of these collections will represent, in a pure sense, a distinctive style, but rather they will represent a distinctive life-style that is intended to capture your imagination and make you want to take the items home. It is today's marketing hook and it is a legitimate, if not an authentic, hook. Today's consumers, you and me, generally fall into either one of two groups. We are either looking for "informal" furniture styles like French Country or English Country or American Country, or we are looking for "formal" furniture styles like 18th Century English, or Regency, or Louis XVI. If you are a fan of the "Modern" you have your own category that looks to me like "informal formal", but that is another story. Do you have to be an expert on furniture styles to be a smart shopper? Absolutely not, but I assure you that the more you know about the styles of furniture that have come down to us throughout our history, the more you will enjoy the furniture items that you buy.

Do furniture styles, either pure or contrived, affect the price of a furniture item? Yes and no. Given today's furniture manufacturing technologies, it is possible to produce almost any style at any price level; however you will generally see certain styles that more often than not gravitate to certain price points, either high or low. As a general rule, the more expensive collections will represent the more authentic reproduction approach to any style. One major exception to this would be the "Arts and Crafts" style which can be found from the most modest price points to some of the most expensive price points, and yet the general feel or look of the items is remarkably similar. Two key elements that formerly differentiated modestly priced furniture from more expensive furniture—carving and fancy veneer work—are no longer the benchmark they used to be. Fancy veneering is still a relatively expensive element; however carving today can be accomplished with master carving machines, able to carve out numerous items in a matter of minutes, and embossing, which allows a manufacturer to create a "carved look" without having to carve each item. What does all of this mean to you? It means that your choices are greater than ever and it means you can have the look you want at almost any price point. Not bad! Throw into this heady mix the dramatic increase in furniture being produced in the Far East and then imported into the U.S. at prices most U.S. firms are finding impossible to beat and you are looking at a "golden age" for U.S. consumers. Get out there into your local furniture stores and outlets and you will be pleased and amazed at the values and looks that are available today.

2

WOOD AND VENEER

How to Spot Quality in Tables and Casegoods

All wood furniture is manufactured in essentially the same way. Quality is in the details, not is some secret technique. The chart on the next page is a typical manufacturing flow chart. Most high-end companies follow this type of program during the manufacturing process.

The only way you can begin to determine the quality of a desired item is to see it in person. You should at least try to see a sample of work produced by the manufacturer. Touch it, and feel the finish. This will tell you a lot about the item. Are the edges smooth? Does the finish feel silky or, if it is a casual finish, is it smooth to the touch? Do the drawers work well? Are the interiors of the drawers smooth to the touch? How is the overall design of the item? Is it out of scale or does it seem too light in scale, or too heavy? Are table legs secure and tight in position? Do the leaves fit well? Do the leaves match? You don't have to be an expert to recognize what is well done. Pay attention to what you can see and touch because these points will indicate whether the item is cheaply made or is a quality product.

How about the price? Won't that tell you if you're looking at a quality item or not? It should; but price is not a foolproof guide because most manufacturers make a wide range of products, utilizing many different manufacturing techniques that often are not apparent. A high-end manufacturer may produce some less expensive products in order to attract a larger consumer base, taking out many extras you might expect based on the firm's reputation. Is this fair? Is it ethical? Almost all manufacturers, in almost all industries, do the same thing. It is a perfectly legitimate

MANUFACTURING FLOW CHART FOR SOLID WOOD FURNITURE

Here is a typical solid-wood manufacturing flow chart. Most high-end companies follow this type of program during the manufacturing process.

1. The lumber is:
   a. Carefully selected.
   b. Air-dried and kiln-dried to about six or seven per cent moisture content.
   c. Rough-cut to eliminate all warps, knots, checks and splits.

2. Clean stock is assembled into dimensional stock of various sizes, glued under pressure, and cut into rough shapes of pedestals, legs, posts, or drawer and frame compoents.

3. These rough-cut solid parts are further refined by band sawing, then:
   a. Shapers contour the rough edges.
   b. Dovetail machines cut interfacing joints.
   c. Boring machines pre-bore holes for dowels.

4. Master carving machines carve up to forty duplicate images at one time.

5. Sanding is one of the most critical operations because the condition of the piece in the "raw" determines how well the finish will look. The wood may be sanded by various belt, wheel and drum sanders, as well as by hand.

6. All parts now ready for assembly.

7. Component parts such as drawers, doors, tops go through sub-assembly.

8. All parts flow to the cabinet room where the final assembly takes place. They are fitted together and thoroughly fastened with dowels, glue and screws, either in combination or as a single procedure.

9. The assembled piece is placed in a hydraulic press to ensure tightly fitted joints and, at this point, further reinforcements such as corner blocks are added.

10. Table legs and leaves are numbered to assure proper fit because these items are shipped flat in a box and assembled at the store or at home.

11. Drawers and doors are fitted properly.

Do all manufacturers go through the same steps? Essentially they do, and this is what makes the process of determining the relative quality of items so tricky. In a brochure produced by the manufacturer, or a color photograph used in a magazine or newspaper advertisement, different brands of furniture can appear to have the same look of quality.

business strategy; but it does demand that you, the consumer, know your stuff. The low-end product from a medium- or high-end producer may not be as good as the same type of product from a less well-known competitor. The second firm's regular price may be well below that of the big name manufacturer's low-priced goods. Confusing? It certainly can be.

It is possible to purchase furniture that has very little or no wood in it. Some manufacturers use a cellulose product to make a panel with a photoengraved finish simulating wood. You can spot this material by taking a close look at it. You'll see the same little engraved dots as in a magazine photo.

THE ART OF VENEERING

The common belief that solid wood construction is superior to veneered construction is just not true. The more elegant and finer standards of construction are five- to seven-ply laminates using rare and beautiful face veneers. Remember, Egyptians first recognized that woods, when sliced from a log or section of a tree, produced beautiful designs. Perhaps, being the first merchants, they also worried about "the bottom line", and must have recognized cost differences. The great beauty of wood is better revealed when it is sliced as veneer sections rather than cut as solid sections. Solid lumber does not possess the strength, stability or beauty of matched veneered panels for building quality furniture. That is a fact.

The chart on the next page gives you an outline of the construction of a quality wood panel, so you can appreciate the care good manufacturers take in producing our finest furniture. If it isn't done this way, it just simply isn't a quality veneer panel. A producer can lay-up a veneer panel with three-ply and a cheap core, but the result is a cheap veneer panel. The difference between good and bad is not a mysterious secret. It takes many steps, each done to perfection, to create a perfect whole. It is possible to cut corners in the production process. And it may be true that some of the steps are not very important, in the sense that the piece will not fall down, but eliminate those steps and you have an item that is just not as good.

BENEFITS OF VENEERED CONSTRUCTION

1. Cross-grained lamination provides greater dimensional stability because movement in any direction is restricted by the other layers.
2. Hand-matching creates beauty not found in solid wood construction and allows a great deal of creativity in arranging patterns.
3. Five-ply or seven-ply construction offers more strength, stability and durability.
4. Modern glues or adhesives resist cracking, peeling, or splitting of the wood layers, which increases the durability of the panel, and eliminates the chance of glue failure, a common problem with earlier-generation glues.
5. Veneer artistry (and it is an art) allows the use of many different species of exotic veneers which create a more beautiful look.

MANUFACTURING FLOW CHART FOR VENEER CONSTRUCTION

1. Core stock or center ply is made of poplar or man-made board.

2. Glue reels and presses are used to:
   a. Glue up solid pieces for core stock.
   b. Apply wood banding to fiberboard for shaping and carving panel edges.

3. Direct steps in making the face veneer:
   a. Selection of the flitch (industry name for the fancy face veneer sections).
   b. Cutting and matching:
      (i) drop clipper—cuts the length
      (ii) shear—cuts the width
      (iii) jointer—joins pieces by glue and pressure
      (iv) splicer—fuses pieces by pressure
      (v) patch table—all defects repaired

4. Fancy face veneers: Hand cut, matched and laid-up for decorative veneer faces. Most common woods used are:
   a. oak
   b. cherry
   c. mahogany
   d. pecan
   e. maple
   f. walnut
   g. burls of all sorts—ash, walnut, etc.
   h. ash

5. Veneer pieces are cut to pattern.

6. Fancy faces are hand-laid and glued.

7. Various types of face veneer matching are selected. The name of the match describes the look:
   a. pie matched
   b. parquet matched
   c. random matched
   d. book matched
   e. slip matched
   f. diamond matched
   g. butterfly matched

8 Adhesion: layers of veneer are sent to the glue spreader which applies the glue to:
   a. crossbands—the different layers
   b. face veneer
   c. back veneer

9 The laid-up panel is placed in a press under four thousand pounds of pressure for two minutes.

Five ply veneer construction
Multiple layers of wood, with the
grain running in alternate directions,
is stronger and more stable than
regular solid wood.

Back

Crossband

Core stock

Crossband

Face

Diamond match veneer

Pie match veneer

Random match veneer

Book match veneer

Burl veneer

Crotch veneer

SOLID WOOD VERSUS VENEER: WHAT'S BEST

I've been asked whether a piece is solid wood or veneered a thousand times. Saying "I won't buy any of that veneered stuff" is, in effect, saying "I want to buy some of that bad solid stuff." Of course, no one means that, but the question is no more relevant than asking if white is better than black, or if sliced bread is better than unsliced bread. I can guarantee you that if an item is produced using solids instead of veneer panels, there is no assurance that this fact alone will tell you anything about the quality of the item.

It is interesting to note that in the past two or three years, more solid wood groups have been brought to the marketplace by large, quality manufacturers who have, for the past twenty-five years, been producing nothing but veneered collections. This, however, is a merchandising decision, and not a manufacturing decision influenced by any information suggesting solid is better than veneer construction.

Whenever this discussion comes up, keep in mind that veneer is only found on tops, sides and drawer-fronts. All other component parts of an item are solid. You should also be aware that solid wood furniture is constructed differently. Solid wood tops, for example, must be allowed to move, and this must be taken into consideration by the manufacturer. Whether an item is veneered or solid is not a question that results in any information about the quality or cost of an item. It really is a "non-question" because it doesn't produce information that will help you make a good decision.

QUALITY CHECKLIST FOR WOOD FURNITURE

If you think you are buying the best product out there, make sure of the following points. If these features don't exist on the piece you want to buy, make sure the price reflects a more modest item!

1. Large cabinets, china cabinets, entertainment centers, sideboards, etc., should have **leveling devices** in the base. Remember, there is seldom a level floor in any house anywhere in the world. Keeping your big items level is important because if they are not level their doors have a tendency to stick.

2. There should be **sash locks** on the table leaves and table base.

3. **Drawers** should work smoothly and should not bind when extended.

4. **Drawer interiors** should be smooth to the touch, sanded and sealed.

5. **Glass shelves** should be thick and have plate grooves. 3/8 inch thick shelves are good.

6. Better-end display cabinets and chinas should have **halogen lighting**, line switches and rheostats.

PITCH PINE.

Did you know that Pitch Pine, perhaps the strongest and hardest of the American softwoods, was commonly used to make schoolroom desks and church pews in the 19th Century?

PLUM WOOD.

Did you know that Plum Wood, a European hardwood, was used whenever possible to produce common furniture items from medieval times until the 17th Century?

SOFT WOODS.

Did you know that some Soft Woods like Pitch Pine and Yew Wood are harder than most Hardwoods? Yep! Yew Wood is almost as hard as Oak which is one of the hardest of the hardwoods!

Quality guide to case goods

Turnbuckle

Parting rail

Dust panel

Drawer guide

Dovetails

Glue block

Drawer bottom

Drawer guide

Drawer side

Rebate for inset back panel

Rear view
A cabinet's back panel contributes to its stability and rigidity.

7. **Hardware:** You can tell a lot about a piece of furniture by checking the quality of the hardware. Upper-end manufacturers use heavier, more substantial, more decorative hardware, the bails are often moveable, and cabinet hinges are usually more intricate.

8. Inspect **hinges** on doors to determine if they are solidly secure and can handle the load of the door.

9. Look for **dust-panels** on case pieces. Dust panels should be wood on the best items. On less expensive items they may be cardboard or may not exist at all. Inspect for dust panels by pulling out the drawer or drawers to see what is under them. Dust panels keep dust and varmints from coming up under the piece and soiling the contents of the drawers. They are not important to the structural integrity of the piece, however.

10. Look at the **back panel**. On the best items, it will be wood. On less expensive items, it may be cardboard. It can also be a fiberboard product and, while this does work and is better than cardboard, look for a wood-panel back on the best items. Check also to see if the back panel is inset into the case, instead of simply nailed on the back edges, because this technique contributes a lot to overall stability.

11. Look to see if the piece has a wood finish or a **photoengraved finish**. Reliable store personnel will tell the consumer if the piece has a photo finish as will the catalog information. Photo finishes are not found on upper-end furniture items and are now little used by any manufacturer. We may see the return of this type of "wood" treatment when the last mahogny log is pulled out of the jungles in South America. It is going to happen one of these days!

12. Look at the **drawer guides**. On the best items they will be wood lubricated with wax. Metal guides work, however, and are not a downgrade. Center guides combining wood and metal, or wood and plastic, or plastic and metal in combination are not found on higher quality goods. Metal side-guide systems are found in combination with plastic or nylon bushings on some fine quality cabinet work.

13. Look at the finish. Look for a **deep, clear finish**, not necessarily a high gloss. The degree of sheen has nothing to do with the quality of the finish. I am convinced that even the most unsophisticated furniture shopper can look at a piece of wood furniture, touch the finish, and then give a fairly accurate estimate of the value of the piece. (I don't mean you will be able to nail the price exactly, but I do think you will be able to judge if it is modestly priced, moderately priced, or expensive. Trust your instincts, they usually will be right!)

14. Check to see if legs of chairs, tables, or side pieces have metal **glides** on the base. These glides are put there by the manufacturer to aid in moving the

Apron

Metal extension slide

Leaf lock

Leveller

Corner block

Apron

**Dining table construction,
viewed from below**

item around the factory during production. However, they do aid the consumer because bottoms of legs might be poorly finished and glides will keep them and any potential finish stains off hardwood and carpets.

15. Any time you look at a dining table, put your hand on the corner and try to move it. If you get lots of **wiggle,** watch out! Either the legs are not properly secured or, if they are secure, the leg assembly is poorly engineered. (Remember: wiggles are only good in Jell-O and exotic dancers.)

16. **Glass table tops** should be made of tempered glass and should be between 1/2 and 5/8 inch thick. Glass inserts should be 3/8 inch thick on cocktail tables, etc.

17. Look for **liners** in silverware drawers of china cabinets, buffets and sideboards.

18. Look for **dining table leaves** that are between 18 inches and 22 inches in width and that are fully aproned. This will give your table a more finished look when it is fully extended.

19. Ask what kind of **table slide** is used. Dining tables must remain rigid when all the leaves are in use. Watertown extension slides are the best available, and are especially important on tables that extend to 120 inches or longer.

20. **Entertainment centers** should have the following: Electrical outlets, cable hook-up, pullout TV swivel trays, "punch-out" back panels, VCR pull-out trays, tape storage trays, album storage and pocket doors. Pocket doors, when opened, slide back into the case and are out of the way, which is what you want.

21. **Large cases,** such as triple dressers, will have a turnbuckle that runs from the top back rail to the lower front rail. You can tighten the turnbuckle to ease sagging caused by extra weight in drawers, which could cause the front rail to bow. Not many manufacturers go to this trouble but it is a plus when they do. Drexel-Heritage does use this system. Ask if others use it as well.

22. **Design:** This is hard to define but it is very real. Does the piece appeal to you? Are the proportions correct? Are there extra details on the case? Are the feet carved? Do the frame and panel doors have molded stiles and rails? Feel the weight of drawers and doors—high-quality furniture has a sense of weight, scale and solidity to it. There are many fine design points in high-end wood furniture that are not necessarily present on more moderately-priced pieces. All of these design elements combine to give you a better-looking piece.

These twenty-two points will help you get a feel for the value of the piece you are looking at, and will help you make a better decision on the item, regardless of the price or discount.

WOOD DEFINITIONS

Use these terms and definitions to impress your wife, husband, girlfriend, boyfriend or designer.

Carving and/or embossing: When you look at carving on a furniture item you should, at least as a point of information, ask if the area was carved or embossed. In all fairness, domestically-produced furniture is very seldom carved by a real human craftsman any more. A few remaining craftsmen still carve the master form that is used to make metal forms, which are then put into master carving machines to produce ten or twenty carved sections at a time. These machines produce outstanding carved sections. Our society just doesn't need a lot of wood-carvers any more, and thus it is a dying craft, but we still want carved items, so machines can produce them quickly in the quantities needed for large production runs.

> **PARTICLE BOARD**
>
> Generally composed of wood chips of varying sizes combined with an adhesive. The smaller the particles, the better the board.
>
> **MDF**
>
> Medium density fiberboard. Better than particle board because it is made up of wood fiber and adhesive. It is denser and flatter than particle board. MDF is used in furniture as a substrate for veneer.
>
> **HDF**
>
> High density fiberboard. Similar to MDF but heavier and more dense.

Chipcore, particleboard, high-density boards: Good or bad? Well, like most other things in this world, they can be both good and bad. If someone told you an item was "all wood", would that really tell you anything? It shouldn't, because "all wood" doesn't tell you anything about the kind of wood used, how it was handled, how it was finished and so on. You simply do not have enough information with which to make an informed judgment. This is the case with chipcore and particleboard. It is a fact that quality items are manufactured using these products because they produce a superior foundation for veneers. These manmade core materials, when well-made, have the advantage of being almost impervious to moisture, thus providing a dimensionally stable foundation for veneer that is not going to move, swell or shrink. This stable foundation will allow veneer to be positioned without any undue tension on it, so that stress on the finish will be minimized, and any chance of the finish crazing, etc., is greatly reduced. Done properly, it is a plus for you. Done improperly, it simply makes a piece of poor furniture. I would bet the piece of furniture you are looking at would have revealed itself to you as poor quality long before you needed to ask if any "chipcore" was used in the manufacture of it.

Crotch, stump, rotary, flat cut, burl, quartered: Terms describing the part of the tree from which veneers were cut. Each will yield a different looking veneer depending on how the wood was cut. (If you are not familiar with the terms, and think they are baseball terms, you might look like some kind of nut when you're shopping.)

Distressing: This wood-finishing term can be distressing to the consumer! What is it? It is all those marks, rubs, gouges, dents, specks, etc., seen on the tops, edges, and legs of wood furniture items. Should they be there? Yes and no. The older the item or the more casual the category of furniture, the more likely it is to be distressed. Many designers and manufacturers use distressing because they feel it adds character to the items. Years ago, my group experimented by producing a number of items in both distressed and undistressed finishes to see what we thought of each. We all voted for the distressing because it added so much more personality to the pieces. It is used often on oak items representing early American or fifteenth, sixteenth and seventeenth-century pieces. Look for it on all traditional styles, less on eighteenth-century mahogany or cherry items, and seldom on contemporary items or modern designs. The exception on contemporary items would be designs that utilize very casual, natural finishes and woods. In short: enjoy it. If you hate it, there are manufacturers who minimize it or don't use it at all.

Dovetailing: This is how every drawer should be made. It refers to the way the back and sides of the drawer come together. If, when you look at drawer sides, you see what looks like a interconnecting saw-tooth arrangement, you are probably looking at dovetailing. It is absolutely the best way to make a drawer strong and lasting. Don't believe that any other methods are as good—they aren't, although there are other ways to lay up a drawer.

Embossing is a quick and inexpensive way to fill the demand for carving. However, embossing just doesn't produce a "carved" product with the precision or sharpness a master carving machine does. To emboss is to press, under a great deal of heat and pressure, a pattern into a piece of wood or leather. It works—you almost have to be an insect to tell the difference. If you do your homework, though, you can tell the difference between a carved item and an embossed one by studying the edges of the carving: If the edge is sharp and clearly defined, you could reasonably bet it is carved. If the edges are rounded and smooth, however, it is probably embossed. Is carving better than embossing? I wouldn't suggest you lose any sleep over this but, if you have a choice, go with carving. It is just nice to know a delicate knife did the work rather than an eighty-ton monster machine that cranks out a hundred legs a minute.

> **HORSE'S GLASS**
>
> A "cheval" mirror, which is a full-length glass pivoting in a wooden stand, means "horse" mirror. I have no idea why.

Finish runs or poorly finished backs of wood items: This is a personal thing with me and, I suspect, with many of you. Here you just bought a wonderful piece of furniture—a china cabinet, perhaps, or a bookcase, or maybe a nice table—and the delivery people are bringing it into your house, when you notice that the back of the cabinet or bottom of the table is unsightly. There are numbers and letters on the back, or sloppy finish material, or runs of finish material—in short, the back or bottom is a mess. Is this a problem? Is this an indication that the manufacturer didn't do the job properly? As much as it personally disturbs me, it really isn't an indication of anything but economy. A manufacturer tries very hard not to add cost to an item if it doesn't directly benefit the consumer. While it would be easy enough for the factory to finish the backs, bottoms, or any other unseen parts of a wood item, it would add cost that an average consumer would rather not pay if the areas are not seen when the object is in use. This is, of course, logical and sensible. I just never liked it. This is one reason why I probably would never make any money as a furniture manufacturer. If you are like me, just be prepared to spend a lot more money and time looking for the very few manufacturers who finish these areas.

Five-ply construction is what you should expect in a good veneer panel. You will find many side panels on wood items are three-ply construction, but the bottom-line is: Five-ply construction is better. It is more stable, which is what you should expect to find in better furniture items.

Glue blocks: This is the small piece of wood that is glued to the bottom of drawers to aid in securing the bottom panel to the edging pieces. Good drawers have glue blocks even though good drawers do not demand glue blocks. Is that clear? Another way of saying it is: Good manufacturers, who are not looking for ways to cut corners, still use glue blocks because they add to the stability of a drawer. With new manufacturing techniques and superior modern glues, glue blocks are not as essential as they used to be, but look for them as a clue to determining how far the manufacturer has gone in order to produce a superior product.

Kiln-dried wood: All quality manufacturers of wood furniture use kiln-dried wood, and it means just what you think it does: The wood is placed in a kiln (oven), and dried down to about a six per cent moisture level. This ensures that the item produced will be very stable, and will not work itself apart over the years. (It also means the manufacturer is working hard to do it right.)

Pie match, diamond match, random match, book match, slip match, butterfly match: The way veneers are patterned before they are laid-up on the item. These terms are descriptive of the look of each approach, so if the top looks like a pie cut up and ready to be served, you know you have a pie-match. See how easy it will be for you to look like an expert? (I might suggest that if you think the top is a diamond-match, but you have just given your sweetheart a two-carat zircon, you'd be safer to mention random or book match when you guess the pattern. There is no sense in getting yourself stuck in an uncomfortable situation.)

Table extension slides: Found on the bottom of table tops. The leaves for your table rest on these slides. Are metal slides better than wood? Not particularly, but it is important to be sure the slides work smoothly and the leaves fit properly. Customers seldom check this until the table is delivered to their home. I suggest you ask to see a table set up with the leaves in it so you can test how well the slides work, and see how the leaves look in the table, before you purchase it. Store personnel may not want to do this because the leaves are usually in the warehouse, while the table is in the store. Well, "phooey on them!" It's going to be your table, so ask to see what it looks like before you have fifty people coming for dinner.

Ten-step, twenty, thirty-step finishes: A designer or salesperson may tell you the finish you are looking at is a twenty or thirty-step finish. What does it mean? Well, it used to mean something. Today, I am not sure, for a lot of reasons. I have to wonder what the manufacturer is counting as steps? With some I know, it could be steps to the water cooler. With others, it could be how many times they move an item around the factory. If you hear this expressed as a benefit, it is probably an indication of how hard the manufacturer is working to produce quality furniture. High-end manufacturers do use lengthy finish systems on many pieces to obtain a certain look. They may glaze, tone, re-glaze, coat, rub, etc. The number of steps in a finish process is not, per se, a guarantee of a beautiful or trouble-free finish. With new finish materials available to manufacturers today, they can produce beautiful finishes with much less fuss than was possible even ten years ago. You don't have to be an expert to recognize a beautiful finish. Just look at it and touch it. Is it beautiful? Does it feel good? If you reply "yes" to both questions, then you have your answer.

Veneer: The top layer, or facing layer, of wood on all large, flat surfaces. You will see more veneered furniture than solid wood items. The thickness of most good veneers is around 1/32 inch. It can be less on some pieces, but if you keep this number in mind you will generally be in the ballpark. Remember, veneers have been around since Cleopatra was entertaining Mark Anthony.

WHAT TO LOOK FOR IN CASEGOODS

When you consider buying casegoods that aren't built following the processes outlined above—watch out—or at least don't expect too much!

The difference between an inexpensive piece and a quality piece is more than one single thing. Instead of looking for a $300 difference in one dramatic spot, look for the thirty $10 differences in a number of different spots. Quality is always a matter of many things done well. To understand my point, compare the least expensive dresser in the store with the most expensive one. You will find that the two share all of the fundamental features: drawers, top, sides, bottom, hardware and finish. Yet, even with identical fundamentals there is a world of difference that you can see and feel in each detail. Again, keep in mind that quality is the details and value is the sum total of all these details, at a fair price.

OF OAK, WALNUT, AND MAHOGANY

In the days of yore, when kings and queens ruled the roost and surrounded themselves with retainers and lesser beings, the world of wood furniture was a simpler place. The forests of England and Northern Europe were filled with mighty oaks; and when a table or chair or chest was needed the cabinetmakers would take to the woods and cut down or gather this noble wood. Using all the skills available they would fashion what was needed by the noble lords to fill their manor homes and palaces. Lesser beings, which included almost everyone else, would scurry about the same forests and use the same wood, but the resulting furniture was sparse and crudely made (but made out of oak it was!). Now I am sure that an occasional apple tree ended up as a chest or perhaps a plum tree became a bed but for the most part it was the oak that all of western Europe dined on, slept on, and sat on. And this practice of using the native woods was true for the rest of the developing world.... whatever tree it was that dominated the local forests was the wood that dominated the utilitarian world of their everyday lives. In Europe and England it was the oak and this was true till about the 1660's. The oak was supreme and this early age of wood furniture is known as the Age of Oak.

Of course with familiarity came discontent. Alas this was a common ailment that mankind seems to have and so the wealthy demanded a new look; a fresh look, a look more in common with their uncommon view of themselves. In about 1660 came the dawn of the Age of Walnut. There was a new sophistication about England and Europe. The nation states were maturing and a rising Middle Class was feeling its oats. There was money to spend and new importance to be shared; or perhaps, flaunted is a better word. All of a sudden oak was passe and the wood of the moment was walnut. Now this is not to say that oak was no longer used as a principal furniture wood. It remains to this day a primary wood for certain styles and designs. But from about 1660 through 1730 walnut reigned supreme, and a wonderful wood it is. Walnut, much more than oak, when cut in special ways has a wonderful grain pattern. Walnut trees also produce in their "crotch" areas, and, when grafted, in the stump areas, wonderful swirl grain patterns that are absolutely beautiful when handled by skilled craftsmen. Walnut trees also produce areas of rapid growth that are called nodules. All trees do this to some extent, but the walnut has a greater propensity for these type of growths, and these convoluted growth areas produce wonderfully beautiful burl patterns that when handled by skilled furniture craftsmen are truly works of art. So it was the walnut tree that allowed a new sophistication in furniture design and execution. Design influences from the Continent greatly influence a switch to this new favored wood and much of the Western European world embraced the new beauty and elegance that walnut made possible.

It is very important to keep in mind when considering the utilitarian items that fill our lives how very significantly the political climate that prevails at any point in time influences every aspect of our daily lives and that includes the items that we fill our lives with. As England moved closer to Europe during the 1600's, in political a sense, European influences changed the way that England saw itself and ushered in this Age of Walnut. Conversely as England and the English Colonial expansion seized the day in the early 1700's, the Age of Mahogany came to be. But it is important to note that the changing tides of fashion were not all fluff, feathers, and politics: economic considerations due to diminishing supplies of walnut and the desire for larger pieces of lumber all came together to create the time for a new wood to capture the scene. Around the 1730s that new, old wood was mahogany.

Mahogany is a wondrous wood. Personally, when I think of fine furniture items I think of mahogany. Mahogany was and is not just another wood. It has characteristics that make it inherently superior to walnut and to oak also. Mahogany is very strong. Hard, heavy, and close-grained, it is very resistant to scratching or marking, and can be wonderfully "finished" without even using varnish. It has all of the beauty of walnut as well as being resistant to cracking, warping, and attacks from woodworms. My heavens, in the past it was a wonder wood and it still is even though today we rarely need its natural advantages. But for all the appeal of this new wood it did not have the surface flash of a fine walnut and thus much of the early mahogany items relied on molding and carving to add interest to the finished pieces. The very fact that mahogany logs and the planks cut from them were so large gave cabinetmakers of the period an opportunity to make dining table tops in new sizes and shapes. The expanding English Empire made mahogany a much more available cabinet wood and with the richness of the Empire increasing with every year the use of mahogany increased along with the might of England.

Today wood manufacturers have the ability to use any commercially available wood in the creation of their furniture collections. Oak is still the wood that is most often used in the furniture collections you see in stores today. This is partially true because it is relatively inexpensive and readily available. The casual styles that are sold today lend themselves to the use of oak with its relaxed and interesting grain. Rarely will you see major collections of furniture constructed using walnut today. It simply is not available in large quantities and thus commands very high prices. Walnut is still beautiful but we will not see another walnut period any time soon. Mahogany is still readily seen in today's stores. Most often it will be used to create wonderful 18th Century collections that still have the formality of the Old World. You will see a great deal of cherry in stores today, primarily used in reproductions of those wonderful 18th Century American collections that are as rich today as they were in Colonial America. Pine is making a big comeback and is often used in Country collections both with wood tone finishes and painted finishes. Rubber wood from the forests of Southeast Asia is used increasingly to produce affordable collections that are quite handsome and, of course, maple is still a very popular wood used in Country collections as well as some Modern collections. Amazingly today the type of wood that is used by a manufacturer has little to do with where that wood grew as a tree or forest. The economies of shipping today make it possible for a manufacturer in China to use woods out of a forest in Europe or America or Canada and still produce competitively priced items. American manufacturers have logs of mahogany coming out of the rain forests in South America. Rubber wood out of India. Oak from Canadian forests. There is almost no locale today that is too remote or costly to provide wood for today's furniture items. This diversity in materials is a plus for today's consumers. We have it all today: variety, affordability, style, and utility. What a time to be alive!

WOOD GLOSSARY

Acacia: Light brown hardwood from Australia and Africa. In ancient times it was used by Eastern nations for religious and sacred buildings, and is still used in churches and special architectural applications.

Amaranth: A South African import, this dark purple-hued wood is very fine-grained with good figuring, much used in contemporary furniture.

Amboyna: An East Indian wood. A rich brown, highly-figured wood with yellow and red streaks, often used for modern furniture items.

Ash: Hard, dense wood, generally blond to light brown in color, with a good grain resembling oak. Very good for exposed parts that require strength and a casual appearance.

Bamboo: A woody plant found in tropical forests, generally used for casual furniture utilizing leather wraps as fastening devices.

Birch: Very hard, fine-grained wood, usually a light brown in color, which takes all finishes well, making it the wood of choice when imitating more expensive woods such as mahogany.

Black Walnut: A beautiful native wood. Over-cutting in the late 1800s has reduced the supply and driven the price to very high levels, so it is not used to a great extent today. However, it remains our most beautiful furniture wood.

Butternut: Sometimes called white walnut because it resembles walnut in all matters except color, it is hard, durable, and nicely figured. Trees are found in all parts of the US. Long favored for carving, it is seldom used by manufacturers today.

Cedar: Very fragrant, with an ancient history of use in furniture. Its main use today is for small chests and drawer-linings (as well as specialty boxes for cigars or pencils).

Cherry: One of the "Big Four of the Furniture Woods" along with oak, mahogany and maple. Cherry is a durable hardwood, reddish-brown in color. Generally available only from smaller trees, it is a challenge for the industry to produce at adequate levels and reasonable prices to meet consumer demand.

Circassian Walnut: Possibly the most handsome of the walnuts—a very expensive dark brown wood with a very curly grain, native to the area around the Black Sea.

Cocobolo: A dark brown wood with a purple cast used, for the most part, in the production of contemporary furniture.

Elm: A creamy beige wood with very little contrast in grain or color. It is hard and dense, yet flexible, utilized for upholstery frames more often than in wood furniture construction.

Ebony: Dark heartwood from an African tree, its principle use is as an inlay in fine furniture where a designer wants a contrast line. In most present-day furniture, this contrast line is painted or silk-screened, which results in a major cost saving for the producer.

French Burl: Often used as a term referring to walnut from Persia/Iran. It has a swirly, wonderfully curly grain that makes it very difficult to use as a veneer due to the tendency of the wood to separate into its concentric patterns. Grafted walnut from the Western US is very similar and has been used to great effect by many manufacturers over the past twenty years or more.

Kingwood: An import from Brazil and Sumatra, it is a dark brown wood with black and golden-yellow streaks, generally used as an accent wood in fine furniture production.

Mahogany: Has long been a favorite of designers, craftsmen, manufacturers and consumers. A beautiful reddish color with magnificent grain patterns depending on how it is cut, mahogany is stable, takes finishes well, and polishes to a high level. Generally imported from South America and Africa, it is now coming under pressure due to environmental concerns for the rain forest's viability. There are three types of this wood, of which only one is true mahogany. Khaya ivorensis (African mahogany), Swietenia macrophylla (Honduras mahogany), and Shorea (Philippine mahogany). Only the Honduras variety is a true mahogany. One of the most beautiful varieties, Cuban mahogany was popular at the beginning of the twentieth century, and now is considered almost extinct. African and Philippine mahogany are considered inferior substitutes.

> **NOT FOR BUGS**
>
> Did you know that mahogany doesn't appeal to woodeating insects? This is another reason why is was so widely used during the seventeenth and eighteenth centuries.

Maple: Blond in color, it is hard and straight-grained, but is also available in curly and bird's-eye varieties. A major, if not the major, wood used in the production of Early American-style furniture as well as contemporary designs. Curly and bird's-eye varieties produce beautiful veneer patterns highly favored by designers and consumers.

Myrtle: A beautiful blond wood used most often as an accent wood in fine wood items.

Oak: Possibly the most important furniture wood, from the very earliest of times used in the production of wood furniture. While there are more than fifty varieties of oak, they all have a very similar look and are very hard and durable. English and French oaks are considered superior to the American variety because of the beauty of their grain patterns.

Olive: A light yellow wood most often used as an accent.

Palisander: A brown wood with a violet cast, it is an import from Brazil and the East Indies and finds its widest use in modern style furniture.

Pine: Once one of the major woods for local production in early America, it was cheap, easy to work, and easy to paint. It was Everyman's furniture wood, and is finding a revival as a casual addition to kitchens and family rooms.

Pecan: A light to reddish-brown wood with pleasing grain characteristics. Firm and durable, it is much used in structural situations but was, in the late 60s and early 70s, also used as a face veneer to great effect.

Primavera: Sometimes known as white mahogany, it is most often used in drawer bottoms and other inconspicuous parts of furniture items, or as a face veneer in less expensive pieces.

Redwood: A handsome wood with a rather uniform red color. Resistant to insects and water damage, it is seldom used in furniture with the exception of outdoor items.

Rosewood: One of the great decorative woods used in the production of fine furniture, it is reddish-brown wood with black streaks. The Brazilian variety, called Jacaranda, is considered the finest variety of this tree.

Satinwood: Light blond wood with a satiny finish and a wonderful grain figure, it is a very expensive import from India, chiefly used as an accent wood in only the finest furniture.

Teak: Can range from yellow to brown. Even more durable than oak, teak's principle use has been in shipbuilding. However, a significant amount of very fine contemporary furniture can be found in teak, as well as fine examples of outdoor furniture.

Walnut: Not widely used by present-day manufacturers, it was one of the principle fine hardwoods at different eras in furniture history. It is a beautiful light brown wood found in North America, Europe and Africa. It has been over-cut, and while it is currently under-utilized, it will remain one of the great woods for fine furniture.

Yew: A close-grained hardwood that is a deep red-brown. An evergreen that thrives in England, it has an interesting grain pattern similar to bird's-eye maple, but is a more costly wood and generally used only as an accent by present-day manufacturers.

Zebrawood: A golden-yellow wood with dark brown stripes. It is most often used as an accent wood.

3

WOOD FINISHING
The Coating Protects and Beautifies the Furniture

Believe it or not, the first recorded wood finisher is found in the Bible. In the Book of Genesis, Chapter 6, Verse 14, God commanded Noah to build an ark of gopher wood, and to cover it within and without with pitch (another name for tar). Pitch had been used for centuries prior to the Bible story to seal and preserve wood against the ravages of moisture and water. It is generally believed that the gopher wood of the Bible verse was probably either cedar or cypress. Both species are durable, resinous woods that stand up well in wet conditions—and from the earliest of times it was recognized that woods need to be protected from the elements.

THE EVOLUTION OF THE FINISH

Early wood furniture was subjected to very damp conditions. Given uneven heating (or often the total lack of a heating system) coupled with wood-eating insects and fungi, it is clear that only in the warm and dry climates of Egypt and the Middle East, or the more moderate climate of Greece and southern Italy, was there any chance unfinished furniture could survive. Not only was climate a major factor in the deterioration of wood products, sunlight itself was, and is, one of nature's great destructive forces. Given time, sunlight will destroy any furniture finish. With these natural conditions, it was clear from the earliest times that wood items had to be protected from the elements. The fundamental point of finishing is protecting the wood. Beautifying the wood was a pleasant bonus.

Pitching was one of the earliest methods of protecting wood, as was "charring"—burning or scorching the surface to a depth of about 1/8 inch to protect the wood from fungal growth and allow it to touch the soil without the rapid decay suffered by untreated wood. Greeks and others used vegetable oils, resins from acacia trees, and turpentine from pines as early types of varnish. Secretions of certain insects from the Far East produced a hard shield coating for wood objects. This product, called lac, formed the basis for great advances in finish materials in the late eighteenth century. Beeswax was readily available as another surface treatment, and for centuries these natural products protected and "finished" wood structures and wood furniture. In more northern climate zones, huge fireplaces emitted large amounts of soot and smoke which, added to these natural oils and fats, provided additional protection, as well as a layer of grime that produced the dark finishes characteristic of early furniture. Animal fats were rubbed on furniture items in an effort to clean them—which worked, to a certain extent, and further protected the surface.

The occasional happy result was a beautifully rich finish with a patina that not only glowed, but also had a deep richness to it. I say "occasional" because most furniture produced in these early years did not survive the rigors of the climate, either indoors or out, or the unruliness of the owners. I am sure they were not treating their furniture with an eye to the future. Our attitude is not much different—many of us still think furniture is merely a consumable item to be used up and discarded when its job is done.

Through luck and happenstance, a few glowing examples of beautifully-preserved wood items have survived to come our way. Without a proper perspective it would be easy to slip into a falsely romantic notion that all old furniture was beautiful and was made better than present-day furniture. This simply is not true, but I'll get to this point later.

TODAY'S TECHNIQUES

Let's take a look at modern wood-finishing, and the events that directly led to our present techniques.

Finishing in the modern sense began in the nineteenth century. Paul Johnson, in his book *The Birth of the Modern*, dates the start of the Modern Era at 1815. Napoleon had just met his Waterloo, and the world was on the brink of an explosion of new ideas, technologies and discoveries. In the midst of all this newness, a lowly insect called *laccifer lacca*, a bug which had been around for a few million years doing his thing, and in all probability will be around for another few million years, was found to have the secret to a wonderful finish material. *Lacca's* secretions had been used since Egyptian times, not only as a coloring agent for furniture, but also as dye and glue. The Romans employed this all-purpose product, called gum lac, and others continued to use it through the mid-nineteenth century—the red

---

WHAT IS PATINA?

The patina is the look a finish has after years of wax, weather and wear. Through the wonders of modern chemistry, "instant patina" is possible; don't confuse this with a breakfast cereal.

coats of the British army were dyed with gum lac. But, when aniline dyeing as discovered, the days of gum lac were done.

I can well imagine the scene at the United Gum Lac Works in Calcutta when the owners learned their investment was worth not a million but a mere hundred pounds Sterling. To re-coin a phrase, necessity was the mother of invention: In panic, the partners put their best chemists onto the job. Mixing a solvent with flakes of gum lac, the chemists came upon a revolutionary new product—shellac. What joy there was on the finish line! Not only did this product give a wonderfully attractive finish to a wood surface, but it also dried within an hour to a hard coat. With shellac used in a finishing system now known as French polishing, the world of furniture was transformed, and furniture manufacturers were able to start thinking of themselves as captains of an industry rather than producers of a craft item.

It is important that I clear up the term **finish.** In fact, I may well have been better off starting with this information; but, particularly at this point, it is important to realize that even though we speak of a great "finish", what we really mean is a **finish system**—a series of steps which, done properly, result in a great finish. Beautiful finishes are the result of many steps, both chemical and physical. So, even though all of us use the term "finish" in a singular sense, it really is a collective word that represents a lot of work.

Two separate approaches to finishes are the penetrating finish and the film finish. Penetrating finishes used to be very popular on Scandinavian furniture made of woods like teak and walnut. You will encounter a film finish far more often than a penetrating finish and, even though the term "penetrating finish" sounds more protective and substantial, the film finish actually offers you the most protection for your wood furniture.

FINISH IS EXPENSIVE

Up to thirty per cent of the cost of upper-end casegoods can be due to the finish system.

The thickness of any finish and its chemical effect on a wood surface are the keys to the protective quality of the finish system. Most manufacturers of commercial furniture—that is, furniture for institutional or office applications—use conversion finishes that are tough and durable. Often these manufacturers will use plastic laminates, instead of a finish system, on the tops of their tables and desks to further increase the durability of these high-use surfaces. Today's medium- to upper-end manufacturers of quality home furniture most often use nitro-cellulose lacquer finishes. This finish system produces the beautiful deep, rich finishes seen on much of the more expensive furniture in our stores. But with the beauty also comes the fact that these finishes often are not as tough as those used on the more economical furniture items. Is this a problem? Not in the average home situation. Now, if you have ten children and five dogs, and run a motor re-wiring operation out of your kitchen, I would suggest you consider yourself a commercial operation and look for plastic-finished furniture. For the rest of us, it will come down to how well we care for the beautiful objects we purchase for our homes.

I recently read a wonderfully scathing indictment of furniture-care products. The book is so well grounded in experience, technical data and good common sense that I want to share it with you. I rely heavily on this book, and the information it contains is important for you to keep in mind. *Understanding Wood Finishing,* by Bob Flexner, is published by Reader's Digest Associates. It is worth your investment even if you are not a woodworker or wood-finisher.

Here is what Flexner has to say about furniture polish:

"Of all finishing subjects, caring for the finish is by far the most misrepresented by manufacturers. Claims range from half-truths, such as 'furniture polish preserves the finish', to outright absurdities, such as 'furniture polish replaces the natural oils in wood'. The success of the furniture polish industry in convincing millions of consumers that there's oil in wood that needs replacing has to rank among the great scams of American marketing.

"Deceptive marketing has shifted the emphasis away from the real benefits of furniture polish as an aid in dusting, cleaning, and adding scent to a room. In addition, some furniture-polish manufacturers have totally misrepresented the beneficial role of wax. Instead of pointing out its long-lasting shine and wear resistance, they've made it into a problem, claiming that it keeps wood from breathing by stopping up its pores, and that it builds up to create a smeary surface.

"Enough confusion has been created to spawn a thriving sub-industry, operating out of antique and home-and-garden shows, which specializes in miracle remedies. This 'snake-oil' business markets essentially the same substances as the primary industry at three to four times the price. Its success demonstrates that there are serious misunderstandings about furniture care."

As a consumer, you should know what factors cause the finish on your furniture to deteriorate. There are a number of causes but the most prevalent are sunlight, everyday wear and abuse and, finally, the action of chemicals upon the finish system. These chemicals can be anything from water to nail polish.

You must either protect your furniture from the above hazards or reconcile yourself to the fact that some day you will have to refinish or buy new. A little common care should keep most household chemicals away from your wood pieces. If there is an accident, it is still possible to touch up most furniture finishes so that even a burn from a cigarette is nearly invisible.

Sunlight: The long-term effects of sunlight upon wood or fabric can be very destructive, although many times it is not obvious. All finishes will fade over time if left in direct sunlight. Short of covering your tables and chairs, there is not much you can do to avoid this fading. Use common sense and keep drapes and window coverings closed during the brightest time of day, and try not to have furniture or fabric in direct sunlight for long periods of time.

Physical abuse: Now this is something we can control, but you must keep in mind that all finishes will be damaged by rough objects and by heat, water, and solvents: the rings on our hands, bracelets on our wrists, glasses taken off and left on a table, coins from our pockets, keys from our cars, and on and on. All of these objects, along with the accessory items we place on our furniture—candle holders, picture frames that sit on tables, ashtrays, ceramic objects, stone objects, a thousand things that we place around our homes—take a toll on wood surfaces.

Chemicals: You can say you don't use chemicals in the house but you do, more than you may realize—wine, vinegar, salad dressing, nail polish remover, glue, smoke, deodorant spray, etc. Our homes are awash in chemicals, both natural and synthetic.

An active program of furniture care at regular intervals can be very helpful in maintaining the beauty of any finish. Most householders use either a liquid polish or a spray polish, such as Pledge, or some type of wax. There are benefits with all of these products.

According to Flexner, wax will provide a longer shine and longer-wearing protection, but liquid polish is a better wood surface cleaner than wax. The bottom line is this: If you want easy cleaning and dusting, use liquid or spray polish, but if you prefer longer-lasting shine and wear protection, use paste wax. I once thought the perfect solution would be to use paste wax first and then liquid polish. However, it just doesn't work that way. If you use liquid polish after using paste wax, the liquid polish will streak and remove the wax. So make a choice, then stick with it.

> **FURNITURE POLISHES DO:**
>
> Add temporary scratch resistance.
>
> Add temporary shine to a dull surface.
>
> Aid in picking up dust.
>
> Clean grease, wax, and sticky fingerprints from the surface.
>
> Fill the room with a pleasant scent
>
> **FURNITURE POLISHES DON'T:**
>
> "Feed" the wood by replacing missing oils.
>
> "Feed" the finish.
>
> Protect against heat, water, solvent, or chemical damage.
>
> Slow deterioration caused by light or oxidation.
>
> *—Understanding Wood Finishing by Bob Flexner, Rodale Press*

FIRST AID FOR WOOD FINISHES

Most problems with wood furniture are finishing problems, and solving them is not as hard as you might think. After saying that, I have to add, if you are like me, I suggest you hire someone to do it—I simply am not good at fixing things, even little things that someone assures me are "easy". So, with this disclaimer as my insurance policy, I will tell you how to handle most routine problems with wood furniture. Incidentally, I have tried several of these tips myself. I'll indicate which ones when I come to them.

A word of warning, these tips are for furniture with a lacquer finish. You can verify that your finish is lacquer by testing whether a tiny drop of nail polish remover softens it in an inconspicuous spot. If you are not sure of your finish, don't try them.

1. **When you have a minor scratch:** Go to a hardware store and pick up what is called a "wax stick" (they will have a whole rack of them) in the color closest to your finish color. These sticks are very inexpensive. All you do is rub the stick into the scratch area, covering all of the scratch, and wipe off any excess material. Then get your furniture polish out and polish the area. This works very well in most areas, but do not do this on the top of your dining table or, for that matter, on any high-sheen flat surface. It isn't going to ruin your finish but the result will generally be a brown scratch instead of a white one and it will still be quite visible. I have been told that the right color shoe polish can be used in the same way but, again, only try this on areas that are not too conspicuous.

2. **When you have a white spot** and don't know where it came from: Now this is one that I have attempted myself. I tried it for two reasons: It allowed me to smoke in the house, and it really is simple. Step one: Light up your cigar, sit in your favorite chair and blow smoke all over the room. When someone yells at you, make the following statement in a firm voice: "I am fixing the white spots on the dining room table." No one will believe you, but your response will be sufficiently confusing to give you time to enjoy your cigar. Step two: When you have a good ash going on the cigar, get out a little olive oil—or, if you don't have olive oil, any oil will do—dip a clean rag in it, flick the ash from your cigar on the spot and rub it with the oily rag. Believe it or not, this works quite often. As soon as the spot is gone, polish the area with your favorite polish. This is the perfect problem for a lot of us. In fact, I am thinking of ways to create white spots so I can attack them when I need a break.

3. **What if the white spots are really alcohol spots?** This is even better than plain old white spots because it allows you to have a cocktail with your cigar and still be able to say you are fixing the problem. You need the drink because you want to moisten the cigar ash this time, and then rub it on the area directly with your finger. If you are not a cigar smoker, you can use paste wax, silver polish, or linseed oil. When the spot is gone, simply re-polish the area with your favorite polish. Now, if you did all of the above and the spot is still there, you can try a little ammonia on a damp cloth and quickly rub the area. If this does the job, polish as above.

4. **What to do if you left your cocktail glass on the table without a coaster under it:** The first thing you do is blame someone else. I have also had success with the old cigar trick we just talked about. Or, if you have a blotter in the house (and what house doesn't have a blotter these days?) lay it over the area you want to work on. Then take a warm iron (not hot) and press the blotter over the circle. Keep doing this and the ring should disappear.

5. **You left the candles burning all night and now you have a mess of wax:** This really isn't such a big problem. We have done it more than once—not exact-

ly leaving candles burning all night, but we've had a party with the doors and windows open, and candles do have a tendency to spill over. All you do is to let the wax get cold, remove as much of it as you can with your fingers, and then use a dull knife (not sharp) to scrape off as much more as you can. Don't dig into the finish. When all that is left is the residue, wet a clean cloth with furniture polish and rub the area. This should do it—and if it doesn't, try your cigar method. Have patience and it will clean up. Incidentally, during an expansive, arm-waving, account of my solution to the world's problems, I knocked a candle over on the carpet. Red wax never comes out of a carpet. We now have a ceramic cat sitting over the problem area and, providing we never sell the house, it is a perfect solution. I just thought I would throw that in for you to file with your Heloise Hints.

These are enough first aid tips for anybody. Remember: when in doubt, have someone else do it. Frankly, when you think of the money you spend on a $30,000 car that sits out in the rain for most of its life, and the money you spend on maintenance for your house, the small amount it takes to keep your furniture looking super is actually very small. Also keep in mind that good furniture is infinitely fixable. Really, there is almost nothing that can happen to good wood furniture that can't be repaired to perfection at prices that will delight you when compared to the cost of everything else in your life.

4

SHOPPING FOR WOOD
Never Pay Full Retail! Never!

Shopping for furniture is often difficult for you, the consumer, because in the normal course of events you don't do it very often. Therefore, you don't acquire the expertise you may have when it comes to clothes, cars, boats, guns or jewelry. No one is confused by the quality exhibited by Timex as opposed to Tag Huer, or Rolex compared to Omega, or a Honda compared to a Nova. We are very familiar with the products we buy often during our lives, but furniture is simply a category of goods we don't buy regularly.

We "know" a Rolex is better than a Timex because the manufacturer told us so in advertisements, and the price tells us so in stores. However, most of us would be hard-pressed to itemize ten significant cost differences between the two products, but we "know" the differences are real and true.

Why are we so comfortable in dealing with a wide range of quality differences in most of our consumer purchases but so unsure of ourselves when it comes to furniture? The biggest reason for our uncertainty is lack of knowledge. The consumer doesn't have the knowledge because the furniture industry, fragmented with so many relatively small manufacturers, has never collectively or individually been able to afford the huge sums necessary for advertising to educate the buying public. Most customers read nothing about furniture except heavy sale/discount advertising in newspapers. Educating the consumer about quality furniture has been left in the hands of the retail salesperson. Since this "teacher" is rarely well-trained by either the store or the industry, customers are generally confused and uninformed before, during and after shopping for furniture. This confusion and lack of education has created a consumer who is more interested in the size of the discount than in the product itself.

HOW TO GET IN AND OUT OF A FURNITURE STORE WITHOUT LOSING YOUR WALLET!

Never pay full retail. Is that clear? Wait a minute, after all of the above, now you say, "Never pay full retail!" What is this all about? To begin with, what is retail? What was the last item you bought that wasn't "on sale"? Sale is a word that has changed its meaning over the years. There was a time when a sale simply meant that a merchant had his store open. Everything was on sale. That's why he was in business: His intention was to sell something to someone. But retailing has changed, and the old words have different meanings. If you are not up on your retail vocabulary, it is going to cost you money. Let's take a look at today's furniture store and see how the typical retailer does business.

The number of independent furniture stores has been reduced drastically over the past thirty years, while the number of outlets for furniture has increased. How is that possible? Because furniture can now be found in stores as diverse as Walmart and Nieman Marcus. Catalog sales of furniture are increasing. We have many national and regional furniture chain stores, Levitz, Art Van, Rooms To Go, Pier 1, Ikea, The Bombay Company, Crate and Barrel, This End Up, Raymour & Flanigan, Ashley Home Stores, and Havertys. At the same time, the local independent's numbers have declined and will continue to decline. Many of the remaining local independents have switched from being old-fashioned general furniture stores to being part of large franchise operations. These franchise operations, closely associated with Drexel-Heritage, Ethan Allen, La-Z-Boy, Thomasville, Expressions, or Norwalk, narrow the local store's merchandising when they become part of a national group.

Large discount operators out of North Carolina, like Furnitureland South, Rose Furniture, and Boyle's, have tremendous impact on all areas east of the Mississippi and, to a certain extent, even on the western retail scene. Sears, J.C. Penny, Macy's—the list can go on and on without even mentioning the antique market, furniture showrooms in many major market areas, local decorator and designer shops, used furniture outlets, or the new combination consignment-and-new furniture outlets.

In short, while the number of outlets has grown, the local retail furniture store (which had been a furniture-education resource for local consumers) has been replaced by slick, large, discount-oriented furniture sellers, often staffed by people with limited knowledge. They are, understandably, pushing the furniture they floor and, while this is what business is all about, it has put a greater demand on you, the consumer, to know more about furniture than you ever needed to know before.

A furniture operation is a low turning, high margin store. What does that mean? And why is it important to you? "Low turning" means that the merchandise the store elects to show, and the inventory carried in its warehouse, does not sell very often. Now, this is not a reflection on the merchandise or on the owner. When everyone in the world will buy a loaf of his bread every week, the baker can afford to make only a nickel on each loaf because he is going to sell a hundred thousand of them. However, if the product is a low turn item like furniture, the merchant needs to make much more than a nickel on each sale simply because he will have so few sales compared with the baker.

Business is really quite simple: Whatever is sold must pay the expenses and leave some left over, called a profit. This profit is essential so that the business can be expanded, and so that something will be there waiting for the rainy days that so often come.

Margin: The difference between what an item costs and what it sells for.

Generally speaking, an independent furniture store must keep the average gross percentage of margin in the high forties. There is an old adage in the furniture business: "The shortest road to hell is to lower your margin."

Slow/low turn goods mean high margins so that the owner can cover expenses and meet other financial needs. Now, while this is fundamental business for the store owner, it is also fundamental business for you to to buy at prices as low as you can, and still get all the product you want and all the service you need.

HOW TO SAVE MONEY IN A RETAIL STORE

Never be in a hurry. Never be in a hurry to select an item, and never be in a hurry to buy an item unless it is priced right. How do you know it is priced right? Since we just learned that a furniture operation is a low turn, high margin operation, we know that the markup is high on any item. In fact, an item in a furniture store is usually marked up at least twice and often two and a half to three times what it cost the retailer. This means an item costing the retailer $1,000 will be priced on his floor from $2,500 to $3,000. The markup can even be higher than this, if the retailer has a product he retails exclusively.

Competition will help keep the prices down, but almost every furniture producer publishes a Manufacturer's Suggested Retail Price (MSRP) based on a two, two and a half, two-point-seven, or three times markup. The manufacturer distributes these price lists to dealers, enabling the retailer to show large mark-downs on a product to give you the impression you are getting a good deal.

Now, it is a good deal if you understand the game they're playing. But it's a bad deal if, by not understanding the game, you make decisions based on the amount of the mark-down, and not on actual merchandise compared item to item with a similar piece.

This mark-down circus is a trap for the unwary consumer because all manufacturers give discounts off the regular costs to retailers, encouraging them to buy and promote more product at certain times of the year. So the $1,000 item is made available to the store at a special cost of $900, but still carries a suggested retail price of $3,000. The retailer could offer this product at forty per cent off, or $1,800 on sale, and still be making a gross margin of fifty per cent. These sales are not available to all retailers, nor are they available at all times but, when they are available, the retailer often passes on extra discounts to the consumer. So, that $3,000 sofa on sale for $1,800 can be a pretty good bargain, because most of the time the retailer will not mark it down below $2,000.

When you ask about this, the retailer will insist this is how the game is played, and say the competition is doing exactly the same thing, and that is true. The retailer believes customers will not come into the store to look at this item if it is marked $1,800 every day. Retailers insist that the consumer must see a percentage markdown in order to know that a price is something special. Is this true? It seems to be, and I can assure you this practice will not change in the near future. But you can change—and that's what this book all about. Never be in a hurry, and don't buy anything that isn't marked down at least twenty or thirty per cent. At least this will get you into the right ballpark.

Now, with twenty to thirty per cent in mind, compare this item with another one you like, one that could do the job for you just as well. Learn to comparison-shop. Don't simply buy discounts. Don't assume fifty per cent off one thing is better than thirty per cent off something else. There is no relationship between the discount and the quality of the item. Compare product, not mathematics, and you will begin to save real dollars, not phony dollars.

WAREHOUSE SALES

Always shop warehouse sales but never buy anything there unless it is at least forty per cent off. Warehouses often contain wonderful merchandise the retailer simply did not sell. If an item on a sales floor does not sell in the first ninety days, or at least in the first six months, it will probably end up in a warehouse sale. The retailer cannot afford to keep anything on his floor unless it is producing sales. Warehouse sale stock is loaded with these wonderful "puppies" (one of the better terms to describe product that doesn't move) along with customer cancellations and defective items. The latter, however, are seldom too defective, and are often quite inexpensive to fix. The retailer may have received money back on a defective item, and did not repair it because he needed the money elsewhere, or because he knew the item was a candidate for a warehouse sale.

Another way for the retailer to fill his warehouse sale stock is to buy "dogs" from his suppliers. Every manufacturer has stock that isn't moving. Selling tired, old, or poorly performing stock to retailers has always been one way to clear it out, and to do a favor for the retailer. The producer sells dogs to the retailer, who sells them along with the store's dogs. Remember that one person's dog can be another person's joy.

Because the cost of the dogs is so low, the retailer can advertise savings of up to sixty, seventy and eighty per cent, but—these are savings off the manufacturer's suggested retail price list. (I often think these lists should be put on the New York Times Bestseller List under "Fiction"!) The point to remember is that you can find some terrific merchandise priced very well at a warehouse sale. Be flexible. It may be more economical to buy a sofa that is not quite the right color, and simply paint the room to make it work. Be flexible. It will save you money.

In any store, check the free services: Delivery, in-house repairs, warranties, free decorating service, return policy—all the services which used to be part of the standard package for furniture stores are now either extras or not available at all. Such services have often been casualties of the heavy discounting that is driving the business today.

Since I began writing this book, some dramatic changes have been seen in the manufacturers' suggested retail price lists. It is no secret that these price lists have bothered many manufacturers and many retailers over the years. Many industry insiders have long considered that these price lists lead to abuse and contribute to dismal day-in-day-out discounting. But a new factor has been added. The Attorneys General in states such as California and Florida have come down hard on several large furniture operations, imposing heavy fines and demanding that deceptive discount advertising practices be stopped. In these two states the rule is simple: Advertise any price if it is a price for which the merchandise has actually been sold. It doesn't matter what a manufacturer suggests the price of an item should be—the price in your town, city or state is the price for which your store has already sold that item. Because of this pressure brought to the marketplace, the use of big-discount advertising has decreased but it is still there. Just be careful!

Consumers will still see comparative prices on sale tags, but it will be less insistent and misleading: "MSRP is $1999, our everyday price is $1499." No big black lines through the price indicating an urgent markdown, just a simple notation that the manufacturer says this is what it should sell for, then the price the local merchant needs to get for it. When these stores do have a special sale, they will attach sale tags and give an additional discount for a limited period of time.

All the new pressure on merchants to tell the truth, so to speak, will work in favor of you, the consumer, if you know your stuff. If you don't, if you still need a big discount tag to fool you into believing that you made a good deal—well, what can I say? You're the type who would not have bought this book anyway.

While everything I have said applies to Florida and California, it might not apply in your state. It is easy to tell if the Attorney General in your state is doing the job for you—look at your newspaper advertisements. If the furniture merchant is shouting that his sofa was $2999 and is now, for a short time only, sale priced at $1599, watch out. This is called a comparison price and is generally frowned upon

STORES CAN'T RETURN

Contrary to what many consumers think, a furniture store rarely can return furniture to the manufacturer. It is a special case when a manufacturer will take back a piece of furniture and, as a consumer, you should not special-order a piece thinking the store can return it if you don't like it.

in California and Florida. Remember, as a rule of thumb, the regular price listed in the advertisement should be the price the item sells for every day. If the item never sells for the "regular" price, then the "sale" price can't be much of a bargain. In other words, if a sofa never sold for $2999, then what kind of sale price is $1599?

Excessive discounts of fifty or sixty per cent or more are warning signals that a store is playing games with you. Discounts in the ten to twenty per cent range can well be a true indicator that the merchant is giving you an extra incentive to come in right away. He is taking a true discount from his bottom line to encourage your business now, or else he is cleaning out slow-moving, damaged or dirty items. You should be interested in this kind of sale. Keep in mind the old adage: If it looks too good to be true, it probably isn't!

Before I leave this subject, there is one manufacturer who has resisted the pressure to produce inflated suggested retail price lists—Ethan Allen. The Ethan Allen management took the high road to fair pricing, encouraging their retail operators to do the same thing. And do you know what has happened? Business is better than ever. There is a lesson here that everyone should learn: Members of the public are not fools and can recognize an honest value. Good for the public and good for Ethan Allen.

> **WHAT IS MSRP?**
> MSRP means manufacturer's suggested retail price. In the furniture industry, these prices usually have no relation to the actual price. A merchant should be the only one who decides the price of anything he sells. He is the one who will go out of business if he is wrong.

ALTERNATIVES TO REGULAR FURNITURE STORES AND FURNITURE DEPARTMENTS

There is more than one place to shop for furniture. Alternatives seldom used by the average consumer are antique stores, used-furniture stores, and combination consignment and new-product stores as well as the new mega-stores like Costco, Wal-Mart, Sam's Clubs, etc. The most common perception of these stores has always been that they carry only junk, but you can fine some wonderful items if you take time to look. What has changed is that inexpensive, but often nicely designed, product from China and other points in the Far East is flooding into the country.

Some years ago, a furniture industry guru told industry executives that furniture will never be perceived by the public as a real value, or as a high-priority purchase, until a real secondary market for furniture product is developed. There is, of course, a well-established secondary market for automobiles, and used guns, fine jewelry, art, etc. All have significant appeal and market as pre-owned but still valuable. Some are even more valuable now than the day they were purchased at retail. Not so with furniture. A furniture item has to be at least a hundred years old before it is considered genuine antique furniture, and with the massive numbers of items being produced in fully automated industrial shops, there is little reason to expect many of today's items will be considered tomorrow's antiques.

Have you ever tried to sell any of your old furniture? No one wants it at anywhere near the price you paid for it. Even though most wood items do not wear out and, if properly cared for, look as good as new, just try getting a good price for them. What has hurt the resale value of furniture is the lack of well-situated, well-displayed resale furniture outlets. Until recently, most people would not go near the average secondhand furniture store. But this is beginning to change, and in the next few years you may see more of the combination new-product and consignment store. The time is ripe for this kind of store, a needed resource for all of us.

Tacky? I just returned from England, where I spent many hours looking through antique shops in the Midlands. The prices being asked for wonderfully old legitimate antiques were staggeringly high. Now the consignment store is not about fine antiques, but it could be about wonderful pre-owned Henredon tables, or perhaps a Baker bedroom, a Drexel dining room, or maybe a Thomasville armoire, all at prices significantly below the price of a comparable new product from each manufacture. I know there can be a market for good, well-cared-for designer furniture, just as there is a significant market for pre-owned designer clothes and for good used cars. It's coming, so keep your eyes open and, in the mean time, look into that interesting old furniture shop. It may be dusty, and it may smell funny, but I'll bet you can find something wonderful to brighten up any room in your house.

Let me digress for a moment and mention something I have said for years—something that people have often misunderstood: "The least interesting component of any room is the actual furniture you put into it." I almost believe the statement as it is written. However, it does overstate my point. I mean to say that even the best item from Baker—when put into a room that is badly lighted, badly colored, and badly accessorized—will not make this poor room look good. Conversely, put the most humble piece of furniture into a room that is alive with color and imagination, filled with exciting collectibles and wonderful pictures, and the humble piece of furniture will look a whole lot better.

Furniture alone does not make a room. A room can make the furniture, however, and exciting, secure people make exciting homes, so stop worrying about what brand of furniture you buy. Start shopping the whole range of furniture outlets for items to express your own excitement and your own sense of security. Guess what! You will save a ton of money and the rooms in your home will look better: Your home will look collected rather than projected, reflective rather than neglected.

Get out there and look around. Compare prices. Don't compare discounts. Don't think "new" is something magic. Magic is often something old. Use your imagination. Retail stores are filled with expensive accessories, but the average home is filled with many things that could become exciting accessories if only they were matted, framed, painted or polished. A case in point: I recently saw an old Flexible Flyer sled hanging on the wall of a store. It was all slicked up and priced at $700! You probably have any number of old treasures in your garage—items that could be hanging on a wall, standing in a corner, or sitting on a cocktail table. Many fascinating accessories are just waiting for someone with imagination to see them differently and make them sparkle.

This is the true way to save thousands of dollars when buying for your home. Furniture is one of the few consumer categories where new is not necessarily better.

In fact, new may not even need to be considered from the standpoint of how best to decorate your room. Although new can be exciting, fun, and a number of different things, it isn't always necessary. Think about that. Do you see the possibilities? Can you see the savings? It sounds strange, but once you recognize that you don't have to buy all new, you are then free to buy new better. That sounds like a Zen statement, but the possibilities open to you when decorating your home are almost endless. You are only limited by your imagination—run with it! You will be amazed.

When deciding whether to buy new or old, remember the points to look for—the keys to quality—are still the same. New or old, nothing changes in the factors that make wood or upholstered furniture good. Good wood furniture does not wear out—it is that simple. Although upholstery fabrics can wear out, and upholstery frames and cushions can wear out; a well-constructed item is worth refurbishing. While it is impossible for a 1957 Ford to be anything but a 1957 Ford, I defy anyone to guess the age of a fine dining table.

The quality of furniture—particularly wood furniture with its almost ageless potential—is a very important point when you are considering its cost. Jewelry, furniture and art are three major consumer purchases that do not really wear out in the common sense of that term. With this in mind, the cost of a dining room can really be prorated over a lifetime of use and enjoyment. A $20,000 car might worth $4,000 in ten years, and it has cost you thousands of dollars each year to keep it on the road, while a $20,000 dining room has cost you nothing more to maintain than an occasional bottle of furniture polish. Therefore, the dining room legitimately costs you less and less each year and, if you prorate it, the cost per year is often insignificant. How many consumer products can you say that about? Not many. And how many consumer products keep on giving, the way a wonderful, functional, fine piece of furniture does? Not many!

Good wood furniture does not wear out!

SHOPPING FOR THE BEDROOM

We all need bedroom furniture, but of all the rooms in a house this may be the one most often made to suffer hand-me-downs or less-expensive new purchases. There is a rule of thumb in the industry that a consumer who buys high-end Drexel-Heritage fr the dining room will then look to low-end Broyhill for the bedroom. Since we seldom entertain in the bedroom, we seem to feel that we do not have to spend as much money on bedroom furniture. There is some logic to this. However, I should remind you that we all spend lot of time in our bedrooms and it isn't always sleeping time. We have to stop neglecting this room.

The most important tip I can give you about shopping for the bedroom is this: Don't skimp on your mattress. Buy the best mattress you can afford. Without trying to be cute, I can tell you we spend almost a third of our lives in the bedroom. Think about that. With this much time invested in this room, it should be a place

Armoire

An armoire holds more clothes than a bureau and takes up less floor space.

where we indulge ourselves. The mattress is the first consideration and it should be a good one.

Did you know that standard sizes in mattresses did not become the norm until the 1950s? Let me list them for you: Twin, full/double, queen, king, and California king.

The California king, which is really only a factor here in California, can be a pain for the newcomer who needs linens for an Eastern or standard king which generally have to be special-ordered out here.

My wife and I recently needed to buy a new mattress and, being small in stature, we decided we did not want a California king. We wanted more width instead of more length, simply because we wasted so much of the length. Well, we got the wider eastern king and we love it! In fact, I can't imagine why the wider king isn't the bed of choice out here for anyone under six feet tall (incidentally, that still applies to most of us). We also got the added benefit of a bed that looks better in our bedroom space. It has given us more room and the opportunity to add a bench at the end of the bed, which looks wonderful in the room. There has been talk in the industry for a number of years about dispensing with the California king. However, to date, nothing has come of this idea.

STANDARD MATTRESS SIZES:	
Twin	39 in. x 75 in.
Full/double	54 in. x 75 in.
Queen	60 in. x 80 in.
King	76 in. x 80 in.
California king	72 in. x 84 in.

Now that I have convinced most of you to take another look at your mattress, I want to move on to the furniture in the bedroom. The bed has become the "signature statement" for the bedroom. Big beds. Elaborate beds. Canopied Beds. Poster Beds. Iron Beds. Brass Beds. All set the mood for the room. Since the bed is the biggest single item in the room, it does dominate the room and sets the whole tone of the room. Technically, I should be calling them headboards and/or headboards and footboards instead of beds, but the term "bed" has come to mean the whole mattress/headboard/footboard combination.

A small aside for you to consider: Even though this will create more work for you when it comes to making the bed, do consider an elaborate bedspread, sheets, and pillow setup. It is such an inviting and lush look, it is a shame not to do it.

Once you have decided on the type of bed you want the rest of the room will fall into place. In present-day bedrooms you rarely have more than two walls on which to place furniture. The bed will go on one of the walls, leaving the other for a dresser or armoire. In many of the large expanded master bedroom areas being built in new homes today, this may not be true, but it is still generally the case in most homes. Closet doors, windows and, often, sliding glass doors to a porch, patio or deck area, have cut down on wall space that once was available. But if you have the wall space, smaller chests and incidental pieces can add a great deal of character to a room.

If your room is smaller, you may elect to go with an armoire instead of a dresser. The armoire will hold as much clothing as a dresser and will generally take up half the space.

I must tell you about the armoire. It pre-dates the dresser by at least a thousand years, harking back to those days of yore when there were no closets and no furniture in any bedroom (except the bed). As the French name armoire indicates, it was often a place for armor to be stored. Another story says that a young girl's dowry was put into the armoire and it went with her to her husband's abode. I like both versions.

Another little legend exists concerning the semainier or seven-drawer chest. This is a charming, narrow, moderately tall chest that can fill a niche just perfectly. The story goes that this piece had its origins as a chest for the garments altar boys wore to Mass in a Roman Catholic Church. In the days when few children could read or write, they needed a chest that would hold vestments, etc., and organize them in a fashion that did not require anyone to read instructions. Thus the semainier: The young boys would simply start at the top drawer and work their way down throughout the week. Today it will provide you with a lovely, graceful chest for small, delicate items. Another name for a semainier is lingerie chest. It almost always has seven drawers, one for each day of the week.

By the way, an aside for the gentlemen, particularly younger men soon to be married or just recently married. (This is wisdom, so pay attention.) No matter how many chests, dressers or armoires there are, or will be, in your master bedroom, you will only be able to use one drawer. That is it, so don't ever imagine that all the furniture your wife requires is going to give you more room for your stuff. It won't happen.

Before I leave the bedroom, I want to relate the story of The Great Bed of Ware. This was a bed! Reportedly the largest bed ever made, it was built in the fifteenth century for the inn at Ware, England. It measured some ten feet wide by ten feet long and even had a large trundle that could be pulled out from underneath the mattress to sleep even more people. History has it that this was no bed simply for sleeping, that it was a bed for orgies. It was so infamous, Shakespeare immortalized it in his Twelfth Night.

What more can I say but this: Don't neglect your bedroom. It is a room where magic happens and it is a room that deserves your very best effort.

TYPICAL BEDROOM PIECES

Dressers: Double and triple, with an occasional smaller version often called a commode. When looking at Americana pieces you will often come across a piece called a bureau. All of these items are from 45 inches to 80 inches long, 18 inches to 20 inches deep, and from 30 inches to 33 inches high. Recently, several manufacturers have introduced a "dresser" that is 53 inches wide but 45 inches high. More a chest than a dresser, it is a pleasing shape and a good size for many of today's smaller bedrooms.

Semainier

These tall, narrow chests usually have a drawer for each day of the week—perfect for lingerie

Great Bed of Ware

This largest of beds may have been built for
frolicking with a crowd.

Armoires: Very popular today, perhaps because of the need for storage with less wall space available. Ten-foot ceilings and cathedral ceilings make the armoire's scale a good selection for many rooms. These chests are 44 inches wide, 84 inches high and from 23 inches to 24 inches deep.

Chests: So many to choose from—look at this partial list:

Victorian high boy dresser	Linen press
High boy	Door chest
Chest-on-chest	Lingerie chest (see semainier)
Drawer chest	Wardrobe

And on and on. Wonderful pieces up to 40 inches wide and 70 inches high, usually about 20 inches to 23 inches deep.

Night Stands: Every bed needs something beside it and a nightstand is the usual choice. However, it is not the only choice. If your room is large, a small chest or table can look very good. Use your imagination. Don't think you have to go the conventional way all the time. Night stands generally range from 26 inches to 30 inches wide, from 16 inches to 18 inches deep, and are usually 25 inches high.

Headboards: Are sized to fit all standard mattresses. Remember, the headboard will make the signature statement in your room: Iron, brass, wood, wicker, upholstered, posters, canopies, headboards, headboards and footboards, sleigh beds (that look like the body of an old sleigh) and so on. You will have a tremendous range of choice when looking for the bed of your dreams. Poster beds come as straight spires or posts with rice-carving, pineapple carving, spirals, square posts, and cannonballs, among others.

Mirrors: All manufacturers make mirrors to go with their collections, but don't think you are limited to these matching mirrors. Again, use your imagination and select an odd but coordinating mirror to add extra zing to your room. There are mirrors with decks, tri-fold mirrors, cheval mirrors, and mirrors that attach to the wall or directly to the dresser. Better mirrors are beveled.

Finally, I want to call your attention to a wonderful book by Alecia Beldegreen. Entitled *The Bed*, and published by Stewart, Tabori & Chang of New York, it is beautifully illustrated with photographs and is a delightful look at beds and bedrooms. Don't miss it.

QUALITY KEY: DRAWER STOPS

Look to see how drawer stops are used. On good quality pieces, dresser drawers will have a wood stop to keep them from pulling all the way out. If metal drawer guides are used, the metal guide itself will have a stop. Pieces of lesser quality will have a plastic drawer stop, often stapled to the top of the drawer.

PINEAPPLES AND RICE

In colonial America, the carved pineapple on the four-poster was a mark of welcome; the carved rice motif was a symbol of fertility.

SHOPPING FOR THE DINING ROOM

Formal dining rooms are becoming increasingly rare. I know there are still millions of them out there, and there will be for years to come, but with lifestyles becoming less formal, the demand for formal dining rooms is decreasing. This is not to say there is less need for dining room furniture, however. The table and chair are still a major need, but china cabinets and sideboards are no longer essential. In the past, everyone wanted a cabinet in which to house and display their best chinaware. With living/dining room combinations, space is often not available for a china cabinet or sideboard. When you have the space, however, it is a real treat to have these important pieces on display. Even though the china cabinet may be less in evidence, tables and chairs are in abundance and are better than ever.

You will see rectangles, squares, glass top tables, pedestal tables, refectory tables, gateleg tables, round, and drop-leaf tables, but perhaps the one most utilized is the rectangular, four-legged table, which can be as large as 74 inches in length and 48 inches wide, sometimes extending up to 140 inches in length. Almost all dining tables are 29 inches high. I would expect that 140 inches, which is achieved using all the leaves, is the maximum length you will find in a retail store or manufacturer's inventory. Tables larger than this generally have to be custom-made, as do the metal or wooden slide mechanisms that carry and support the leaves. Remember what we have already learned—top manufacturers generally make their leaves 18 inches to 22 inches in width. The best leaves have aprons, to continue the line of the table but, more importantly, to cover and shield slide mechanisms from view. Don't forget we also learned the best slides are Watertown, the finest metal slides made. Wooden slide mechanisms were, of course, standard on all eighteenth-century pieces and you may still see them on fine reproductions. This is perfectly acceptable, but if you are buying a table that has a large extension, a top-quality metal slide mechanism ensures the stability of your table. I also suggested earlier that you have store personnel set up the table with all the leaves in it, before you buy, so you can see how stable the table is when fully extended, and how well the leaves match.

Some large tables have double pedestal bases, particularly if they are an eighteenth-century period item but, as a rule of thumb, any pedestal table will be less stable than a legged table. This does not mean you should avoid a pedestal table, but rather that the top may have a little more wobble than you want. You will see fewer oval tables today than you would have ten ye ars ago but, as with many fashions in our lives, I am sure they will be back. With the strength of the Country Style today, you will see a fair number of round dining tables. You may see some with diameters up to 60 inches but most will be in the 44-inch range. When you look at dining room items in stores, many will be shown in a display with a china cabinet and, while china cabinets are not selling at the rate they once did, they still make any dining setup look better.

FROM HUNTBOARD TO CREDENZA

A huntboard or hunt table was originally used to serve drinks and food after a fox hunt. With the addition of drawers, it became a sideboard. Take away the legs and add drawers and/or doors built to the ground, and you have a credenza. Add a closed top and it is a china cabinet. Add an open top and you have a buffet with a hutch or deck. If the top is much narrower than the base, and is enclosed, it is a breakfront.

Parts of a chair

Finial

Crest rail

Back splat

Seat rails

Back post

Stretcher

Front leg

Remember, when you have a dining table in your home always use placemats, at the very least, under your dishes. The best protection for your table top, however, is a custom table pad ordered from the store. Table pad manufacturers have, on file, measurements for all top quality producers' most popular tables, so it will be very little trouble for store personnel to order a pad for you. They are not expensive and are worth every penny.

WHEN SHOPPING FOR DINING ROOM FURNITURE, REMEMBER TO LOOK FOR THE FOLLOWING:

1. **Tables** that are solidly built. Look under them to see how well the legs are secured and fitted into the top. Push the table from an end to see how stable it is. If you get a lot of wiggles, watch out!

2. Look for high-quality **metal slide mechanisms.** Watertown slides are best. Wooden slides are not necessarily bad but look them over carefully and question your salesperson about them.

3. Look for **aproned leaves** 16 inches to 22 inches in width.

4. **Glass shelves** in a china cabinet should be at least 3/8 inch thick and have plate grooves in them. Make sure the cabinet has leveling devices in the base so that it can be leveled for your home.

5. **Chairs** are the major cost in any dining room group. Make sure they are put together in a quality manner. Look to see if the front legs are glued, screwed, and corner-blocked. Dining chairs suffer a lot of stress on the back legs, which should be one piece of wood from the bottom of the leg to the top of the back rail. If the chair is light in scale, it almost certainly needs stretchers on the legs.

   Dining chairs will have either fully-upholstered seats or slip seats. Fully-upholstered seats will be the most expensive since each chair is upholstered individually. The slip seat allows the manufacturer to make the seat at another location and bolt it on just before the chair is crated. By the way, slip seats can be a real plus, allowing you to change your seats at any time for very little money and fuss. Most chairs today will have slip seats, but you'll find fully upholstered seats somewhat more comfortable.

6. Servers/serving carts: You will not see as many of these on display as you would have ten years ago. They function just as the names suggest. They are small, doored, or doored-and-drawered chests, often with a heat-resistant flip top or sliding top. With large casters for ease of movement, they were a wonderful addition to the dining room. If you have room in your dining area, consider these wonderful side pieces to add that extra touch and function to the room.

When selecting dining and family room pieces, keep your lifestyle in mind. If you fall in love with a wonderful eighteenth-century dining room with its typically high-sheen (high-gloss) finish, you must be prepared to pamper the tabletop. If your lifestyle does not fit this kind of finish, you should consider a low-sheen, rugged, natural finish that is much more forgiving. The worst thing you can do is try to re-build Tara when your lifestyle is Suburban Soccer, Basketball, Dance, Bar-B-Q, School Play, Model Airplane, NRA, and Friends of the Condor. Tell yourself the truth about where you are "at" and most furniture troubles will disappear. All, that is, except the payments.

SHOPPING FOR LIVING ROOMS AND FAMILY ROOMS

The formal living room is disappearing from the American scene, and is being replaced by the family room. In reality, the only things that have changed are the terms we apply to these rooms. Prior to the 1950s the term "family room" wasn't used. The family gathered in the living room for all functions not specifically reserved for other rooms, but with the 50s came television and the TV dinner—and the living room was doomed. Alas! But, since we really haven't lost anything more than terminology, we should rejoice in the fact that today's family room can be just that—a wonderful gathering place for the family, in which to enjoy one another and to enjoy all the gadgets we have in our homes today. Since it is the most-used room in the house, it is important that we make the family room perfect for our needs.

ON THE WALL

The Shakers usually hung their ladder-back chairs on pegs on the wall. This got the chairs out of the way while they scrubbed the floor.

In present-day homes, this room is most often adjacent to the kitchen. The original purpose was to keep Mom in the equation and allow her to oversee the activities of children, pets, husband, friends, committees, etc., while doing "kitchen" kinds of things. In short, the family room, now sometimes called the "great room", is the hub of the house. Let's take a look at what goes into the average family/great room.

It must be comfortable. Think about it: If this room, which is going to be used constantly by the family as a whole, isn't comfortable, you have wasted your money. Your first priority must be comfortable seating space for everyone. If you can't do this, the whole idea of the room falls apart. If you have a family of five and only provide comfortable seating for three or four, where do you think the other person is going to be? Whatever your answer, it is a good bet that person will not be with the family in the family room. Now, I know it is difficult to imagine five people who want to be in one room looking at the same show, listening to the same music, or trying to read a book when the noise level is high. It can seldom be done, but if the first step—providing enough seating for everyone—isn't done, then it will never happen.

Keep this in mind when you think about seating more than two people: No matter how big your sofa, you will never get more than two people on it at one time unless you are having twenty people over for a committee meeting. It just won't happen. So don't think a sofa will take care of three or more. In fact, you may not even need a sofa. What about five chairs? Remember, there are no Furniture

Police. No one will ever arrest you for doing something out of the ordinary. When it comes to your home and your furniture, do what makes you happy and do what works for you! If you do, you will never make a mistake.

After decisions about seating are made, figure out what other items you need for the room. Good lighting is your next concern, and that generally means tables for your lamps. If you don't have room at every seating spot for a table, consider floor lamps. Wherever you have a seat, you need light and a place to put drinks or snacks, bringing you right back to the comfort concern. Make this room "people-friendly". If you have space in the room for a party table (25 inches high) with four good chairs around it, you can make the room even more functional. If a party table won't fit, think about a smaller round table with small chairs. Bookcases are always a super addition to the family room and, if you have room for a great cocktail or coffee table, you will add even more look and function. The idea is to maximize the space so that all of you can pursue whatever activity relaxes you or whatever interest nourishes you.

A final word on the family room: When you choose upholstery, make sure you carefully select fabrics that give you the most comfort and the least fuss. Leather is always a super selection for high-traffic heavy-use situations. However, if leather is too expensive or is just not your thing, then take a look at the new synthetics. They will give you lots of look and lots of tough wear. After all that, go ahead and enjoy yourselves!

The entertainment center is often the focal point of the family room. This is not surprising given the great strides that have been made in television and recording technology. With TV screens of up to 60 inches delivering sharp, wonderful pictures, with the digital recording of music and with videotapes, the chance to be entertained in your home with theater-quality sound and pictures is at an all-time high. Today's family room offers you not only a family gathering place but also a multipurpose room full of tremendous opportunity. With so many activities taking place in this room, it is essential that we maximize both comfort and function.

Let's look at the entertainment center first. Prices for entertainment centers range from a few hundred dollars to several thousands of dollars. With this much price spread, it is clear that almost anyone can build a room around this item, which is not only physically large but also activity-large. Since the least expensive entertainment center will usually consist of open shelves and posts, it is not necessary to worry about some of the inherent problems peculiar to the more closed-in expensive pieces. The most important element to consider is heat buildup from your electronic equipment. All entertainment centers should have an open back, or a punch-out panel in the back, to vent heat buildup. Now, this heat is not enough to set your house on fire, but it is significant enough to damage the finish on wood, and will not be particularly good for equipment, either. So look for this feature. An open back

NO FURNITURE POLICE

You won't be arrested for furnishing your home to suit yourself, no matter how unconventional your tastes. Do what works for you!

also lets you position overscaled equipment so that it doesn't stick out the front. If this is the case, it will stick out the back—but that generally is not a problem.

Another important element to investigate carefully is the construction and operation of any pull-out shelves for the TV, VCR or other components. It is essential that these shelves, which often incorporate a rotating mechanism for positioning components, can carry the weight of your electronic equipment. Don't guess when it comes to this, or you may find your TV in a pile near the fireplace or sitting in someone's lap. And, because these shelves telescope out with only the rails and anchoring plate holding them, be sure to check the security of these areas.

Stores that sell a lot of entertainment centers will usually have staff who are quite helpful in determining just what you need. It is important, in more expensive centers, that the manufacturer wire the piece for electricity. Each separate unit, and there are often more than one, should have its own plug-in area so you can make connections from one unit to another. This will save you much grief when installing your equipment.

If you haven't checked lately, it seems that an average setup has a million feet of wire. All these wires hang down the back, and this is reason enough to buy a center with a back on it. All of the more expensive centers will have pull-out storage for tapes, records, CDs, etc., as well as concealed areas for speakers.

I have a surround-sound setup in my family room and, except for two small speakers behind me in the rafters, and the "boom-box" (my children insisted) behind a sofa, I just don't see any speakers—they are all built-in.

Pocket doors are a real plus in an entertainment center. These are doors that retract back into the case out of sight. If the doors on a center simply swing to the side, they will be certain to be in someone's way sooner or later. Look for pocket doors—you will be glad you have them.

Closely related to the entertainment center is the computer center and they share a common utilitarian function: an item of furniture that seeks to organize all the components of a family of gadgets. Unlike the entertainment center I think the computer center is a waste of money and a poor solution to creating a work station. I know we are talking about the home and the term "work station" may be a stretch but let's face it: people who need and use a computer need a better work area than the computer center gives them. In my home office I have a large four piece desk top that holds all of my office needs; tower, monitor, printer, scanner, fax machine and I still have a large area to spread out my papers, etc. Trust me you can't work well when all your components are crammed into a box that is called a computer center. Buy a multi-piece, wrap-around desk set-up and you will have a good, functional, work area that will hold all your equipment. I bought my set-up from Office Max and I love it. I even loved the price: I don't think I paid more than $400 for everything. OK, OK, there is one unique "computer furniture item" that I think is essential and that is the "section" that has a drop-down shelf for your keyboard. Absolutely essential for me. Bottom-line for computer centers! A waste of your money.

OK, we've spent all this time on the family room—but what about the actual living room? Well, if you do have a living room, so much the better. Think about making this space a quiet retreat. Don't make it a stiff, formal area that waits, neglected, for a major event. Of course, if you are stiff and formal then make it stiff and formal. I am sorry if I offended anyone, but my point is this: Use the room. How often do you meet someone whose living room looks like a static display at the local museum? Too often. Don't waste this space. Since everyone is using your family room as a high-energy high-impact room with lots of activity, you can go into the living room when you want to escape.

WARRANTIES ON WOOD FURNITURE

Frankly, you are not going to hear a lot about warranties on wood furniture. Low-end or less expensive producers of wood furniture rarely talk about a warranty, and upper end producers—who could talk about lifetime warranties if they wanted to—never do. I know that several years ago Drexel-Heritage hd a five-year warranty on their wood product, but I am not sure if they still offer it.

The problem is this: What are they going to warrant? The finish? We have already learned that sunlight and oxidation change all finishes on all wood pieces, no matter what they cost. Since manufacturers cannot control how a product will be handled in the home when it comes to sunlight, it is impossible to warrant against this problem. The same can be said for oxidation. This leaves us with the way the item functions. No matter how badly it is treated, the function of a piece of wood furniture is seldom impaired: A dining table can still function as a dining table even if you've played soccer on it. It won't look good, but you could still have your dinner on it. So a function warranty is not practical. What it boils down to is this: In all the years I spent in the furniture business, I never knew of a single problem that either the store that sold the furniture, or the manufacturer that made the furniture, did not correct. It may require a letter to the president of the company, but someone who feels badly used is usually only too ready to write a letter.

The furniture industry, both retailing and manufacturing, is the most pro-consumer industry I have ever seen. In fact, it is pro-consumer to a fault. Sadly, not all consumers are honest about what created the problem they have with an item of furniture that is not right for them. But even with this blatant deception, which happens occasionally, the consumer complaint is, in almost all cases, handled in the consumer's favor.

One reason for this is that the manufacturer works very closely with the retailer to ensure every item of furniture delivered to a customer has been "deluxed" by the retailer: Each piece of furniture that comes out of the manufacturer's crate is run through the retailer's back room touch-up, repair, and deluxing program. Any

FEATURE OR DEFECT?

Differences in wood grain and color aren't defects. They give character to a piece of furniture.

problem should be caught at this point. Does it always happen? No, but it does with almost all good retailers. This is part of their cost of doing business. Any problem not discovered in the back room becomes far more expensive to correct after the item is delivered to your home. So, as you can see, everyone has a big economic incentive to do it right the first time.

Consumers are sometimes confused by the term "open stock". Furniture salespeople may tell the customer that an item is open stock, implying that the piece will always be available from the manufacturer. However, the manufacturer will only produce a line of furniture as long as it sells well enough to warrant its production. So, if you purchase a dresser, mirror, and two night stands, today and go back in six months to buy the five-drawer chest from the same collection, you may find the manufacturer has discontinued the group. Some furniture collections can be in production for five, ten, even twenty years. Others may have a life span of only one or two years.

One of the biggest complaints from consumers is that different items from the same collection do not match. Often it will be a color match problem or a veneer pattern problem. We know that wood finishes are always undergoing change due to sunlight and other factors, so that an item produced in January may have a slightly different tone than a piece produced in September. It is extremely difficult to ensure that all items being delivered to a customer came out of the factory at the same time. This simply is the nature of a business that deals, for the most part, with organic materials. Almost all wood problems could be eliminated if all manufacturers went to plastic veneers or plastic solids. Absolute matches could then be expected. But the wonder of wood furniture is that it is so varied and unique. Differences in wood grain and color that bother some consumers should really be looked at as character—a plus, not a minus. However, this is again a question of education and generally most problems begin with the information flow from the furniture salesperson to the consumer. By not being completely honest (rarely intentional) and by not explaining the wonders of a natural product, a salesperson will leave a small percentage of consumers unprepared for what they receive. This is the basic cause of most problems. Let me leave it at this: I don't believe you will ever have a problem with the furniture you buy, from any good retailer, that won't be corrected by either the retailer or by the manufacturer of the merchandise. I believe they will even take care of you when you are wrong. I know, because I have seen it happen repeatedly. Relax. Furniture will be your most trouble-free experience in consumer purchasing.

5

·······

UPHOLSTERY

Color and Comfort on Display; But Quality Is Hidden Underneath!

Color and comfort are the key elements upholstery items bring to a room. Quality in upholstered furniture begins with the frame, which is largely hidden, and ends with the fabric, which is all that most people ever see. Let's take a close look at these high-impact pieces of furniture and see what they are all about.

ERGONOMICS, PSYCHOLOGY, AND UPHOLSTERY

Ergonomics is the study of the relationship between human physiology and the physical environment. This relationship, coupled with the psychological impact of color on any human being, makes the selection of upholstered items much more complicated than selecting a wood item. Rarely do we consciously consider ergonomics or psychology when buying furniture for our homes, but the fact is we do pay a great deal of unconscious attention to feelings and colors. We aren't always aware that we consider these factors, but we do consider them very intently, which is why we make comments like, "This chair just doesn't feel right," or "I'm uncomfortable in a green room," or "I don't want too much color in the room."

Even if you are not making a conscious analysis in your selection of a piece of furniture, you are certainly making unconscious decisions based on how the item affects you. This is why color and upholstery selection for your home can be so tricky—especially when, as in most cases, you and your wife, roommate, or husband are in on the selection process together. Another influential factor could be a foolish designer or decorator who is trying to do your room based on his or her own impressions instead of yours. This is something you don't want and, in all fairness, I must say you won't run into this type of egomaniac too often.

With all this in mind, let's take a look at upholstery and see what we can learn.

QUALITY CHECKLIST FOR UPHOLSTERY

1. **Air- and kiln-dried lumber**: This is very important. If you don't have a quality frame it will not matter how expensive a fabric you put on it. The item will simply be of inferior quality, and will not stand up to any wear and tear. Increasingly many of the better producers of higher-end upholstery are using laminated panels when making up their frames. This is not a short cut or a mark of inferior construction; but like every other element in the production of furniture you can do it well or you can do it cheaply. Keep your eyes open and ask good questions.

2. **Back pillows**: These should be generously filled with a quality filler—dacron, feathers, down, etc. Whatever the filling, it should be soft yet resilient, and have a good recovery factor. This means that when you get up, the pillow will "come back", or recover its shape. You may still need to fluff it a bit, but it should need only a minimum of help to look good again.

3. **Cushions**: Similar to back pillows in the sense that they should be generously filled with good fillings, polyfoam cores, poly-down cores, dacron wrapped poly cores, or spring down cores. All of these cores are good (depending on the source, of course) and these represent the majority of types available today. Unwrapped foam cores are not quality cores, but poly-foam cores that are a part of a cushion package (poly-foam wrapped with dacron and encased in a down-proof tick) make excellent cushions.

4. **Individually selected coil springs**: Carbon steel springs—individually selected as to tension factors, i.e. using heavier gauge springs in the center of the heavy seating area, and fanning out with lighter gauge springs reflecting different weight-load conditions—are a hallmark of quality. These indicate that the manufacturer is working very hard to ensure the best possible comfort level for the sofa or chair. Does this mean the item will be right for you? Not necessarily. Buying upholstery is like buying a pair of shoes—some fit and some don't. The fit has nothing to do with the quality level or price of an item.

5. **Marshall spring unit in the back**: While this is a nice feature, it should only be used in tight-back sofas or chairs. Rarely, if ever, will it be used on a loose pillow-backed sofa, because the pillows supply the comfort and the added thickness of the Marshall unit is not desirable.

6. **Chamfered frame**: This simply means all of the sharp edges of the frame, over which fabric or cord will be applied, will be shaved off, providing a

QUALITY KEY: SCREWED AND GLUED WITH CORNER BLOCKS

Legs should be screwed and glued to rails, with corner blocks for extra insurance. Remember: Legs that are simply screwed or nailed on are not, cannot, will not be a plus for you.

QUALITY KEY: CURVED FRAMES

If the sofa has a curved back, the frame must be curved. If the arms are curved, the frame must follow the contour.

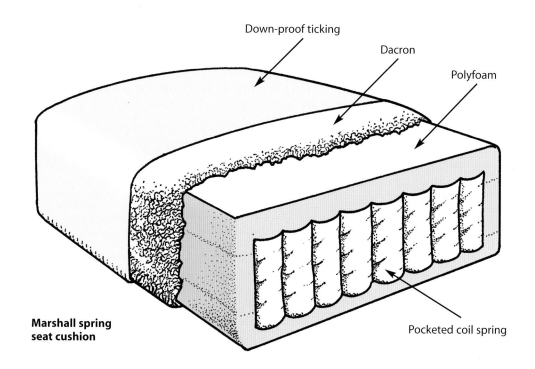

Down-proof ticking

Dacron

Polyfoam

**Marshall spring
seat cushion**

Pocketed coil spring

nice smooth surface that will not cut the fabric, or increase wear on these surfaces.

7. **Shaped and contoured frame:** Means the upholstered shape of the sofa is also the shape of the frame. Curves or contours will not simply be padded in, with no support. This is very important because a shape that has no frame integrity will quickly lose its looks.

8. **Selected hardwood frame:** Provides durability and dimensional stability. If the frame isn't hardwood, you could have serious trouble. Some lower-end manufacturers use softwoods such as pine, fir and hemlock. This does not constitute quality construction. Up above I mentioned that more and more laminated panels are being used in the construction of upholstery frames. This is neither good or bad. Techniques change all the time in every industry.

9. **Sateen deck:** Plain-color, tightly-woven deck cover, usually color-coordinated with outer upholstery fabric. It is generally conceded that putting the outer or major upholstery fabric on the deck is a waste of money, and it also increases wear on the major cover due to the cover-to-cover contact. No major upholstery manufacturer "self-decks" (uses the same fabric on the deck as on the over-all frame) unless you request it. Don't request it. It will do nothing good for you or your upholstery.

10. **Legs:** Back legs of a sofa or chair should be a one-piece unit—one piece of wood that extends from the top back rail to the floor. A leg should not be

simply nailed or screwed to the frame. The front legs of a sofa or chair should be screwed, glued, double-doweled, and corner-blocked into the frame, then this frame should be clamped under pressure to ensure a tight and secure fit. A well-made frame should never fail. Never. Any good manufacture will guarantee a frame for life. Fabric and filling materials wear out. Frames should not.

11. Another mark of quality will be **synthetic filling materials** believe it or not! Some oldtimers, often superb craftsmen, may still like to use horsehair matting and jute webbing. In a one-of-a-kind custom situation, where price is no object, these traditional materials may still be used. It is OK, if you are sure of the reputation of the upholsterer. Almost all large, upper-end upholstery producers use synthetics today, not to save money, but to provide a non-allergenic, odor-free product that will also be mold- and mildew-free. As recently as the '60s, upholstery produced in the South could, on a hot August day, smell like your old dog. It didn't happen often, but it only had to happen a few times to drive a manufacturer mad, not to mention the consumer.

DAVENPORT TO DIVAN

Some names for the common sofa are: Davenport, chesterfield, couch, and divan.

THE FRAME IS FUNDAMENTAL

The fundamental element that determines value and quality in an upholstered piece is the frame. Think about it. The frame is like your skeleton. It is like a home's foundation. If the frame can't carry the other components, or if it is cheaply done, the sofa or chair simply can't be good for the long haul. With a cheaply-made frame, an item can be adequate for certain applications, and it can certainly function as a "starter" item but the price should reflect its humble origins. It should not be priced over $800. One of the basic points I want to make is: It is good business—for you—to carefully consider what you are trying to accomplish with your furniture purchase. For example, don't pay more than $800 or so for a sofa for your vacation home but, at the same time, don't ever expect it to be as good as a sofa that looks similar but sells for almost $2,000. It just isn't so.

Let's take a look at what should go into a frame. The best frames are constructed from lumber that is 6/4ths (one and a half inches) or 5/4ths (one and a quarter inches) thick. Elm, maple and hackberry are the preferred woods. A quality frame should be constructed using only a single wood species. Elm, maple and hackberry all have similar characteristics. They make very "clean" lumber, i.e. free of knot holes and other imperfections. They are all strong and hold staples and screws well. All the lumber used in a frame should be kiln-dried to resist warping and "racking" (twisting). The back legs of a chair or sofa should be the exposed ends of a rail (a single wood member) that runs from the top back rail or arm rail of the item, but the exposed front legs of a quality item or the legs of a skirted item are often made out of

TAKE IT EASY!

The easy chair originally was developed for the old and infirm. It was a needed addition to the home, given the low comfort level of most chairs at the time. Early easy chairs almost always had winged backs. In a house without central heating, the wings helped keep the drafts off.

mahogany or other fine woods. This is OK if—and this is a big "if"—the front legs are glued and screwed and double-doweled into the front corners.

All of this will add up to a frame that will be stable for years, which is very important if you are spending over $1,600 on fabric (or more than that for good leather) that could have a life span of more than twenty years. If the frame isn't done right, it doesn't make sense to cover it with a fine leather or fine fabric that could conceivably outlive you.

No matter what a salesperson tells you, screw-on legs are used because they are easy and inexpensive for the manufacturer to produce. They are not what you want.

When a quality frame is assembled with the above-mentioned features, it is laid-up (put together) using wood dowels, screws and glue and then clamped together in a device that puts great pressure on all points and secures all of the sections together. The screws are driven home and the frame is then secure. Once the frame is assembled, it must then be prepared for the application of cushions, back pillows, springs, and any other feature that the designer has engineered. These steps are the only way to do it right. There are a lot of ways to do it wrong—and you will discover them all if you simply buy low price.

One important note on the frame before I move on to the other elements that constitute quality in an upholstery item: The shape of the frame should be determined by the final shape of the item. Inexpensive sofas and chairs are often produced using one standard frame—a rectangle or a square—that the manufacturer then pads into the required shape. This works—until the item comes into use. The only way a sofa or chair can retain its shape is for the frame to follow the final contour of the item. Ask your salesperson about it because, if the frame is not the same shape as the item, it is not a high-quality piece.

After the frame has been properly constructed, it must then be prepared to receive the springs and padding on which cushions and back pillows or tight backs will be positioned. In the best applications of padding and spring-up, the frame is fitted with sheet polypropylene secured to the frame by staples. This material is somewhat elastic and provides a soft foundation for the padding, cushions, pillows and fabric. Without this underlayment, these materials would simply slip through the large open areas and provide no support or comfort to the final product. Producers of inexpensive items use thin cardboard in these areas, and while it may work to keep the padding in place, it is certainly the least satisfactory method.

One of the main reasons for using good techniques when padding the frame, is to cushion any area that will rub against the final upholstery fabric. This rubbing would, in effect, cause the fabric to wear from the inside out! Keep in mind that you and your partner will be dropping hundreds of pounds of weight into the sofa or chair every day. This will cause all the elements of that item to flex, move, compress and stretch, causing wear and abrasion on any element that is not padded or engineered well. This factor is one of the main reasons why inexpensive items wear out quickly. Not only are they stressed on their outer surfaces by wear, dirt and neglect, but their internal structure is also stressed because the undersides of the fabric are getting undue wear.

A very subtle touch by the best producers when engineering all aspects of padding and fabric wear is that they will even go to the extreme of chamfering (rounding off) the edges of wood members that have spring ties or fabric riding on them. These are the little touches that go unnoticed, and generally unannounced, but they are the touches that produce the very best product.

Today, in most cases, padding is made of dacron or a similar fiber. This filling is used in all open areas, and to cover all areas that will be covered by the final fabric. Not only does this pad the item, it also adds a layer of thickness to produce the lush contours so desirable in present-day upholstery.

Before we get to the pillows and cushions, we must talk about the springs and spring deck (the area under the cushions where the springs or spring device are positioned in the chair or sofa.)

> **DID YOU KNOW…**
>
> that our term "Cab", as in taxicab, comes to us from the French word "cabriolet" for a carriage that often had a chair seat with a "cabriole leg" that we still see used often on chairs and tables in stores today.

THE EIGHT-WAY HAND-TIED DECK

In the best and most expensive items, the springs rest on an interlaced arrangement of propylene webbing straps. These go from front to back and from side to side. The springs are placed on this foundation, clipped to it with insulated clips to reduce the potential for noise, and tied with poly twine to each other and then to the rails of the frame. This, when done properly, is called an eight-way hand-tied base, or deck.

The eight-way tie has become a hallmark of quality in the trade. However, its definition has been so stretched you can hardly take it to mean anything of value when comparing one item to another. "Eight-way" has never been a protected tradename or even a technique demanding strict legal protocols. Almost anyone can use the term—even if they just drive eight different ways to work in the morning, or tie one spring eight ways and the rest six or four ways, they still call it an eight-way tie. The unit in question can also have a machine-tied eight-way system. In short, what used to be an important indicator of quality is now almost no indication of anything. You will find retailers selling different sofas, priced from $700 to $4,000, claiming they all have eight-way hand-tied spring decks, when many of them have no such thing.

However, the question may be of little importance today for a number of reasons besides just the corruption of the term. In all fairness—and most importantly—present-day materials and techniques make the eight-way hand-tied system less essential than it used to be. In the days when natural twines were used to tie the springs, it was found that these twines would dry out, rot, or be eaten by the house

Polypropylene padding

Helical coil springs

Wood frame

8-way tie

8-way hand-tied deck

Each spring is held in place by ties to its neighbors, to the edge wire, and to the frame.

Edge wire

Front rail

Donkey dick

Polypropylene padding

Deck

mouse, so a system was needed to ensure that, when the twine failed for any reason, the position of the spring would remain the same. Therefore, the eight-way system came into being virtually as an insurance policy to keep springs in position. Manufacturers who used natural twine found that eight ways worked far better than four or six, but ten was overkill—thus the eight-way hand-tied system became a hallmark of quality.

Now the ties used to secure springs are almost always a polypropylene product, and simply do not wear out, rot, smell or get eaten. They just don't fail. However, top upholstery producers still use the eight-way hand-tied spring deck, primarily to control the way the item "sits"—by utilizing different springs in different locations and tying them together into an integrated system that meets their standards, they can make a more comfortable sofa and a better quality product. This is a very important quality point—the best manufacturers use heavier springs towards the center of the frame and a lighter-gauge spring near the front edge. The producers of less-expensive items are simply looking for ways to cut labor costs, and this is an area in which they have a great opportunity to really cut down on labor.

So—look for the eight-way tie, but don't be a slave to it. Today it is simply one of the multitude of features that make the difference between the best and the rest.

> **DID YOU KNOW...**
>
> that a "Rest Bed" is another name for a "Day Bed"? It means just what you think it means: a place to rest during the day!

6

BUYING UPHOLSTERY

Choosing the Right Fabric Is the Most Expensive Decision

What is the difference between a sofa that costs $2,000 or more, and one that costs $1,000 or less? They often look remarkably alike. This is the dilemma for the upholstery-shopper. Most key quality features are covered up by the fabric, so merely looking at upholstered furniture is not enough. You must be armed with enough essential information to be able to ask the right questions, to look for clues indicating quality and, finally, to trust your body to tell you if it is comfortable. We are going to see exactly why there can be such a price difference between apparently similar items.

PRICING UPHOLSTERED FURNITURE

Before we can fully understand the discount practice in the furniture industry, we must understand what a retail price is. In the best sense of the term, a retail price should be the price any product will bring in the marketplace. This is simple enough, and it is true. However, there are factors which determine this marketplace price:

1. **Demand:** As you can well imagine, if there is no demand for a product, that product will simply not sell. Let's consider a five thousand-dollar heating unit for a home in New England. It may well be a "hot" item at $5,000, but the same $5,000 heating unit, offered for sale in the middle of a tropical rain forest, would probably not sell for $100 as scrap iron. There would be no demand, therefore there would be no sales.

2. **Competition:** The second most important factor in any retail price is competition. I'll use the same heating unit as our example: If the producer of the heating unit had three competitors, each of whom sell the same type of unit for $4,000, you know the producer of the $5,000 unit would go out of business. Who would pay a thousand dollars more for the same type of product? No one, except the mother of the president of the manufacturing company.

SITTING AND LEANING BACK

Cushions are what you sit on, pillows you lean back on, and bolsters are usually small throw pillows which are additions to many sofas.

These are the two biggest factors in determining the price of anything in the marketplace. It doesn't even matter if a manufacture can't make a decent profit from the sale. The marketplace will only be willing to pay the price of the least expensive product that meets all the needs of a majority of buyers. The manufacturer will either be content with the resulting profit or he will not continue production. Business is really very simple. It is hard to compete in this business world of ours, but the rules ultimately are very simple: Produce at a price that the market will bear, and at a cost that permits you a profit. If your product can't fit these basic criteria, then it is doomed.

CUSHIONS AND PILLOWS

We now come to cushions, which are generally the second most expensive component of an upholstered piece (after fabric). For the most part, there are five different types of cushions: foam, dacron-wrapped polyfoam, poly-down, spring and down, and all-down or twenty-five per cent down with seventy-five per cent polyester. Rarely will you find any other type of cushion on present-day items. Let's take a look at each one individually:

QUALITY KEY: INSIDE THE CUSHIONS

All cushions should have cores that are sewn into muslin or down-proof ticking prior to insertion into the final upholstery fabric.

Foam: A foam cushion—usually found on only the most inexpensive items—is often flat. It quickly loses its support and often its shape.

Polyfoam: The dacron-wrapped polyurethane core, in a thousand variations, is today's standard cushion and can be very good. It also can be not so good, depending on the quality of the materials. You will find variations of this cushion on sofas priced from $700 to $3,000. When it is made correctly, by a good producer, it is an excellent cushion that should give you years of wear.

Poly-down: The poly-down cushions—with a polyurethane core and a wrapping of down mixed with poly—will give you a very deep, comfortable seat. These cushions can give your sofa or chair a very relaxed, casual look.

Spring-down: A spring-down cushion is one in which the core is a configuration of small lightweight springs encased in muslin, then surrounded with a wrap of down materials. Spring-down was the first variation from the all-down cushion, which was prized by those individuals who had parlormaids constantly fluffing cushions and pillows on sofas and chairs. In an effort to get away from these high-maintenance cushions, which were very comfortable but needed lots of attention, the spring-down cushion came into being. Not only was it comfortable, but it would also "recover" (spring back to shape on its own). In today's world poly-down cushions have taken the place of spring-down for most producers. However, you can still find the spring-down and it can be very good. Don't avoid it, by any means, but be prepared for it to be a more expensive option.

All-down: Although most consumers should go with polydown, you can, of course, still get all-down or twenty-five/seventy-five down cushions. Rarely will you see either of them sold as standard on any item shown on a retail floor, but they can be special-ordered for many of the best and most expensive upholstered items today. However—unless you are used to all down, or simply like the luxury of it—I don't recommend that you spend extra money for it. (All-down is an acquired taste, like caviar, and my question is: "If you have to work hard to enjoy something, why do it?")

Pillows are easy. Almost all the back pillows and throw pillows you see in stores are filled with dacron or a similar product, or with a combination of dacron and down.

As you've already read, well-made cushions will recover well when you get up from a sofa or chair. This means the cushion itself will spring back to its original or intended shape without fuss. (Oh, it may need a little help, but not much.) The same can be said for pillows. All well-made cushions and back pillows will have core materials encased in a muslin-like fabric. This is done for several reasons, one being that almost all cushion cores used in the industry are made by a few cushion-core manufacturers to each producer's specifications and thus need to be in a form that can be handled and shipped to the producers. In addition, it makes for a "cleaner" and more consistent cushion seat. Muslin or down-proof ticking on good quality cushions also reduces wear on outside upholstery fabrics. Another benefit is that it will help to keep the cushion in alignment. The welts will not crawl, nor will the cushion lose its shape.

> **QUALITY KEY: A SOFT FRONT EDGE**
> Most upper end sofas, when the skirt treatment allows, will have a soft front edge to the deck. This front edge will have a large rolled welt, known to old-time upholsterers as a "donkey dick".

FABRICS FOR UPHOLSTERY

We now come to the most expensive single element of any sofa or chair—and that is the outer fabric. As you well know, fabrics can range in price from $3 a yard to $300 a yard or more, and fabric selection can dramatically affect the final price of an item. The fabric you choose can more than double the starter price of almost any sofa or chair.

Nothing changes except the fabric selection and yet the price can double. How is that possible? All producers of upholstery will offer a fabric line that fits their pricing structure. This allows them to calculate the cost of producing any item in their line with any of their selected fabrics. With this information, they are able to print the price list shown to you when you are making your decision.

From the mill

Railroaded

Railroading

A fabric is railroaded when it is turned ninety degrees from the direction in which it comes off the bolt. If the mill weaves a stripe vertically in the bolt, and it is applied to the sofa horizontally, then it has been railroaded. Railroading is most often used to avoid seams.

Most high-end producers will allow a customer to select any fabric from any source and have it used on one of the producer's frames. This is called COM (customer's own material) or a similar term. It almost always represents an increase in cost to you.

In determining the price of a fabric used on an upholstered item, a major factor is the amount of waste that results when the fabric is cut and matched according to the producer's upholstering standards. Depending on the fabric, there can be waste factors of up to fifty per cent or even more. This means that if the sofa normally takes fifteen yards of plain fabric to upholster, it will take an additional seven or more yards of patterned fabric to do the same sofa, which is why there are vast price differences between two pieces that appear, to the consumer, to be the "same" sofa.

There is even more fabric wastage when the manufacturer uses four-way pattern matching, which requires additional material in order to line up the patterns properly from top to bottom, from right to left, and inside and outside. The four-way method is the most expensive but is also the most pleasing to the eye.

All of these cost factors are avoided by the producer of inexpensive sofas and chairs, whose fabric selection will be limited to mostly plain types of fabrics. When the low-end manufacturer does have to match a pattern, a center match (putting the main pattern interest in the center of the cushion and pillow) will be used, and only on the inside of the item. This method cuts the amount of waste to almost zero and thus is a major cost reduction. The "inside" of an upholstered piece consists of the top and inside arm, cushion and pillows. The "outside" areas are the back, outside arms and skirt base.

It is very important, in any discussion of fabric, to realize there is little or no correlation between what a fabric costs and how it will wear. In fact, there is almost an inverse relationship between cost and wear. Often the most expensive fabrics are the least durable—silks, damasks, expensive wovens and the like—can be very fragile and vulnerable to marking and abrasion. For tough, almost indestructible wear, you need to go to nylon frisé. This is the fabric you used to see on sofas in the lobbies of old movie houses. (This fabric will be discovered in some landfill three thousand years from now, by a scientist who will then attempt to describe our society by extrapolating backwards what we must have been like to have developed such a tough fabric.)

It is an absolute—price will not tell you how well something will wear or clean. Watch out when you are choosing the fabric of your dreams. Let your head rule and not your heart.

The right fabric, correctly selected for the use it will get as well for as its eye appeal, will save you lots of money and lots of grief. This is what upholstery is all about. Decisions can be very complex and very emotional because your eye and your psychological makeup push you toward certain color selections

FABRIC GRADES

There is no industry standardization of fabric grades. A fabric in Drexel may be grade "F" and an identical fabric in Highland House a grade "10". Manufacturers can grade any way they wish—numerically or alphabetically, with names, names and numbers, or even names and letters.

QUALITY KEY: HOW FABRIC MATCHES

Better or higher-end (more expensive) producers will usually match the fabric pattern in their upholstered items using a "four-way match".

and certain textures. Be armed with the facts, and you will make excellent choices that will not only please you but also save you significant amounts of money.

A final note concerning upholstery: Whenever possible, have your purchase treated with a soil repellent. There are many such treatments on the market, and reputable retailers carry good products. These treatments should be guaranteed by the manufacturer of the treatment. They will help keep your upholstery clean and are worth the cost—treating an average sofa should cost no more than $100.

CHARACTERISTICS OF TEXTILE FIBERS

People working with upholstery are often asked the question: "How will this fabric wear?" It is a very hard question to answer. While it is true that every fabric and fiber has certain wear characteristics, it is also true that the wearability of any fabric is, to a great extent, determined by how it is used. Identical sofas or chairs can have dramatically different wear lifetimes when used by dramatically different owners. Therefore, the consumer really does need to know what to expect from a fiber and thus from a fabric. Here is a brief rundown on the most common natural and synthetic fabrics. (A more detailed list appears in the glossary at the end of this chapter.)

PLANT FIBERS

Cotton: Widely used, it is very versatile and economical. It does soil very easily, so I strongly recommend that you always have cotton treated with a soil protector.

Linen: Not widely used as an upholstery fabric because of its tendency to wrinkle, it is seen in prints and contemporary fabrics.

ANIMAL FIBERS

Silk: Luxurious and relatively fragile. While silk can be long-wearing, it is not a fabric of choice for high-traffic situations in the home.

Wool: We are seeing more wool in upholstery situations. It is very versatile and a high-quality, good-wearing fiber, cleans well and wears well. It is more and more often blended with other fibers to improve the "hand" as well as to increase the design opportunities. It used to be employed frequently in contemporary fabrics such as those used on Scandinavian styles.

SYNTHETIC FIBERS

Acetate: Acele, Avisco, Celanese, Chromspun, and Estron are trade names for this economical upholstery fiber. It does have a tendency to fade in heavy sunlight so watch it. It is not very good used alone and should be blended with other fibers.

WELTS

Cording, piping, and trim are all known as welts in the industry. This is the piece of fabric (preferably cut on the bias) that defines the edges of cushions or pillows. The welt can also be made from a fabric that contrasts with the main fabric of the upholstered piece, thus the term "contrasting welts".

Many synthetics are used in blends with natural fibers to produce better-wearing, more economical fabrics. Often these blends produce wonderful new patterns of color and texture that are not possible when a single fiber is used to produce a fabric.

Acrylic: Acrilan, Cresian, Orion, Zefran are trade names for this fiber that often appears wool-like. It cleans up well and is finding increasing application in upholstery fabrics.

Modacrylic: Dynel and Verel are trade names for this fiber similar to acrylic. It is even more soil-resistant than acrylic, and can be used to great advantage when creating fur-like fabrics. You will see it most often in the home as faux fur throws and rugs. (By the way, modacrylic rugs and throws are fire-retardant if you want to have one in front of your fireplace for those winter events!)

FABRIC TIPS

Never put a striped fabric on a channel-back sofa or chair.

A heavy fabric will not make an acceptable shirred skirt.

Bear in mind the relation of the fabric pattern to the frame size.

Never use a bold plaid or stripe on a tufted piece.

Nylon: A.C.E., Antron and Cordura are trade names for this, the "granddaddy" of the synthetics. It can have a silk-like texture and is often blended with other fibers to create wonderful fabrics. It does have a tendency to fade in sunlight but it is widely used in carpeting, as you well know.

Olefin (polypropylene): Herculon and Vectra are trade names of this fiber widely used in upholstery fabrics. Very economical and very soil resistant but presents a problem in strong sunlight. Olefin is never used in formal settings—it is a more casual look, often woven into plaid upholstery fabrics. (Early efforts had a tendency to "pill" and I remember, more than once, having to "shave" a cushion or two to keep a customer happy.)

Polyester: Dacron, Fortrel and Trevira are trade names for this workhorse of the furniture industry. Widely used for cushion fillings, it is really today's substitute for down. It can have either a silk or wool-like hand and has given the present-day manufacturer a tremendous "do all" kind of fiber with any number of applications.

Rayon: Avril, Enka and Zantrel are trade names of this other "grand-daddy" of the synthetics. Another economical substitute for silk or cotton. Most often seen as a blend with other fibers to produce upholstery fabrics, it is made from cellulose which occurs naturally in plants. (Paper and cellophane are also made from cellulose.)

Triacetate: Arnel is the trade name of this fiber, which is seldom, if ever, used for upholstery fabrics. I included it because you will see it when you look at drapery fabrics.

Microfiber: Is the new buzz word in the world of fabrics. It is a polyester product that is woven so fine that it is described as a "microfiber". It isn't even new but the impact that this new, old fiber is having on the furniture world is spectacular. You will run across the term most often when you are looking at the new suede looks on furniture floors.

PLASTICS

Vinyl: Naugahyde is the trade name for this widely-used leather substitute. Vinyl often gets a bum rap for something that offers so much economy at a very decent look. When the need is there, it is tough to beat this material. Great for dinette seats and commercial uses, easy to clean and available in a multitude of colors. It is not, however, a substitute for real leather because it does not offer the wearability, feel, smell or breathability of leather.

PVC: Saran is the trade name for this, vinyl's fellow-plastic. Not often used in upholstery, it has applications in shower curtains and wallpapers.

> **DID YOU KNOW...**
>
> that the first "Plastic" was produced in 1862! Several of our most influential furniture designers, Eero Saarinen and Charles Eames, utilized plastics in furniture design using plastics developed in the 1930's.

Rarely will you run into a fiber that we haven't identified here. Most fabric problems for the consumer occur because of improper fabric selection. Logic would say to you: "Don't put a fine silk fabric on the chair you will be using when you watch TV," but it is done far too often. If you really think through the uses for which you need the upholstered item, and then buy accordingly, I can promise you that eighty per cent of your potential upholstery problems will never develop.

RANKING UPHOLSTERY MANUFACTURERS

If you are unfamiliar with this industry, the following list may be of help to you before you shop for furniture. Note: I have not ranked these manufacturers in any order other than Good, Better, Best. Before I begin this list it is very important to note that there are many, many manunfacturers that I have not mentioned. Really far more than I have mentioned. Why then didn't I? Keep in mind that I am listing those manufacturers that you are more likely to run into in stores across the nation. Please feel free to contact me at www.newfurnitureideas.com for information on any manufacturer that you do not find mentioned and I will be delighted to research the manufacturer and comment on them for you.

THE BEST UPHOLSTERY PRODUCERS

Baker	Marge Carson
E.J. Victor	Century
Henredon	Tomlinson
Heritage	Stickley

GOOD UPHOLSTERY PRODUCERS

Drexel	Pennsylvania House
Thomasville	Flexsteel
Sherrill	La-Z-Boy
Ethan Allen	Ferguson Copeland
Highland House	

BASIC UPHOLSTERY PRODUCERS

Bassett	Sealy by Klaussner
Simmons	Guildcraft
Lane	

Upholstery, more than wood furniture, is often produced in local markets by small producers, with quality ranging from fair to outstanding. The cost of setting up an upholstery operation is only a small fraction of the cost of producing wood furniture. For this reason you can find in your local market (particularly large markets like LA, New York, Chicago, San Francisco, etc.) the whole gamut of quality production. Don't hesitate to investigate any local shop that has an excellent reputation. Don't be a slave to national brand names when it comes to upholstery. You may have "the best" right around the corner.

I have neglected to discuss the wholesale showrooms that represent the smaller custom-producers of upholstery, and I did this intentionally, because I am talking to the vast majority of consumers—those who do their shopping at retail. It almost goes without saying that those fortunate few who can afford to shop for the very best will get the very best from those select producers geared to create one-of-a-kind items. May we all have that problem some day!

CARING FOR UPHOLSTERY

Keeping your upholstered items clean is more of a challenge than keeping your end tables clean, but it really isn't a big problem. My best suggestion is for you to keep it dusted well. Remove those pillows and cushions and clean behind them. Keep the crevices clean. Wash your hands often (this will also keep down the number of colds in your family) and don't let anyone sit in your good furniture when wearing garden clothes, gym clothes, or what-have-you clothes. If you do all of the above, you are really doing all you should. If and when your upholstery needs cleaning, it is best to let a professional cleaning service do it, rather than handling it yourself. And remember, it is rarely a good idea to spot-clean upholstery. While you may clean up the spot, you are often left with a bleached or faded area that is just as obvious as the spot was. Always have the entire piece cleaned at one time. You will be happy you did.

For your own information, and to pass along to your cleaning service, consumers should be aware of the coding system developed by the Joint Industry Upholstery Standards Committee. The committee seeks to have all upholstery manufacturers code their fabrics with a letter, and attach cleaning instructions to every item.

In most cases, the store at which you bought your upholstery can give you this information, or they can get it for you. If they don't have any information on the recommended cleaning method, or don't want to get it for you, I would suggest that you cancel the transaction and leave the store. You don't want to do business with an organization that either doesn't know the facts or is dealing in such shoddy merchandise that the manufacturer doesn't conform to industry standards. Leave, leave, leave! There are many other good stores that will work hard for your business.

Here are the codes and recommended cleaning approaches developed by the Joint Industry Upholstery Standards Committee:

"W"   Only clean this fabric with the foam of a water-based cleaning agent to remove over-all soil. Many household cleaning solvents are harmful to the color and life of a fabric. Dry cleaning by a professional furniture cleaning service only is recommended. To prevent over-all soil, frequent vacuuming or light brushing is recommended to remove dust and grime.

"WS"   Clean this fabric with shampoo, foam or dry cleaning solvents as desired. Do not saturate with liquid. Pile fabrics may require brushing to restore appearance. Cushion covers should not be removed and dry cleaned.

"S"   Clean this fabric with pure solvents (petroleum distillate-based products, Carbona, Renuzit, or similar products may be used) in a well-ventilated room. Dry cleaning by a professional furniture cleaning service only is recommended. Caution: Use of water-based or detergent-based solvent cleaners may cause excessive shrinking. Water stains may become permanent and impossible to remove with solvent cleaning agents. Avoid products containing carbon tetrachloride, as it is highly toxic. To prevent over-all soil, frequent vacuuming or light brushing is recommended to remove dust and grime.

"SW"   Clean this fabric with a water-based cleaning agent or with a pure solvent in a well-ventilated room (petroleum distillate-based products, Carbona, Renuzit, or similar products may be used). Dry cleaning by a professional furniture cleaning service only is recommended. To prevent soil, frequent vacuuming or light brushing is suggested to remove dust and grime.

"X"   Clean this fabric only by vacuuming or light brushing to prevent accumulation of dust or grime. Water-based foam or solvent-based cleaning agents of any kind may cause excessive shrinking or fading.

THE UPHOLSTERY WARRANTY—DOES IT EXIST?

Unlike wood furniture, upholstery items often feature a warranty. You will hear from salespeople, and read in newspaper ads, that this sofa or that chair has a "lifetime warranty" on the frame. Sometimes you will even be told the fabric has a one-year warranty, but it is rarely more than one year, and is offered by very few producers. Interestingly, I don't think any upper-end manufacturers have fabric warranties.

In general, you will not get a warranty on the durability or color-fastness of a fabric. Why not? For the same reason I mentioned when we were looking at wood furniture—there is no way for a manufacturer to monitor or know the conditions under which the product was used. It is difficult to control the amount of sunlight coming into a room, and sunlight can be the biggest problem a fabric faces. Fabrics fade. In fact, they can be guaranteed to fade. The only variable factor is how quickly they will fade. Another factor that makes a warranty doubtful is the wear any one fabric will get—for instance, a sofa in fabric A sold to customer B could wear well and look good for twenty years. The same sofa, in the same fabric, sold to customer C, could be a shambles in three years. Why? Because customers B and C each have a different agenda for the sofa. Kids, dogs, cats, and lack of care will see the sofa beaten up quickly, whereas two adults who travel frequently and have no pets will often close up their home and, therefore, have a sofa that is rarely used. How does the company warrant a product when there is so much variation in use? It can't. That is why fabrics are seldom warranted.

Another problem for manufacturers is the cost of a fabric and the resulting expectation level of the customer. When you pay $3,000 for a fine sofa in a beautiful silk and find that it looks bad after a year, you have a problem. Remember this: There is often an inverse relationship between the cost of the fabric and how long it will wear. The more expensive the fabric, often the more fragile it will be and the shorter a life span it will have. Don't make the mistake of thinking expensive fabrics will wear better. If you have a rough-and-tumble world to contend with, look for tougher, less expensive fabrics. You will save yourself not only money but also a lot of grief.

Having said all that, I must tell you there are many expensive fabrics available that will give excellent wear, for example, many heavy tapestry fabrics, and those manufactured with the rainbow warp system. There are a lot of durable expensive fabrics but again, expensive does not necessarily mean long-wearing.

Careful selection will eliminate most of your potential problems. If you select properly, the only thing left to remember is sunlight in your room.

And a final thought: Always, always, always have your dining chair seats, as well as your upholstery, treated with a soil repellent. You will be glad you did.

FABRIC GLOSSARY

Appliqué: A pattern that is cut out, then sewed or pasted onto the surface of another material.

Batik: The pattern of a fabric is covered with wax and then dyed. The wax is removed after dyeing, producing a white pattern on the dyed background. This process is repeated to make multicolored designs.

Bouclé: Woven or knit fabric whose surface is looped or knotted. This term is derived from the French word meaning "curled" or "buckled".

Brocade: A class of rich, heavy, jacquard-woven fabrics with raised floral or figured patterns. The look is emphasized by contrasting surfaces or colors.

Brocatelle: A fabric similar to brocade, but with designs in high relief. It is made on a jacquard loom with a satin or twill figure on a plain or satin background. The pattern has a distinctive blistered or puffed appearance.

Calender: To press cloth so as to produce a smooth, glossy or other special finish.

Calico: A term formerly used for a plain, woven, printed cotton cloth, similar to percale. The name is taken from Calicut, India, where it was first made.

Cambric: A plain weave soft cotton or linen fabric calendered with a slight luster on the face.

Canvas: A general classification of strong, firm, closely-woven fabrics usually made from cotton.

Cashmere: A soft wool textile made from Indian goat hair. The same breed of goat is now found in the United States, Europe and South America.

Chenille: A type of woven yarn which has a pile projecting all around at right angles to the body thread. Think of your bath towel.

Chiffon: A sheer, gauze-like, silk fabric.

Chintz: A glazed, plain-weave cotton fabric decorated with brilliantly colored figures, flowers, etc.

Corduroy: A strong, durable fabric with a cotton ground and vertical cut-pile "stripes" formed by an extra row of filling yarns.

Crewel: Embroidery using wool worked on unbleached cotton or linen. It was widely used during the Jacobean period for upholstery and drapes and recently, during the 1960s and 1970s, for use on wing chairs.

Damask: A broad group of jacquard-woven fabrics with elaborate floral or geometric patterns, generally made from linen, cotton, wool, silk, rayon, etc. The pattern is distinguished from the ground by contrasting luster. Damask is reversible.

Denim: A heavy cotton cloth of a twill weave. Think of your blue jeans.

Duck: A canvas-like material that is often given a protective finish against fire, water, etc. Early rainwear manufacturers used this material.

Embroidery: The art of decorating a material with needle and thread. It is thought to have originated in Italy during the sixteenth century, probably to give ladies of leisure something to do.

Felt: Material made by matting together, under heat and pressure, woolen fibers or cowhair, etc. Your father's hat was felt.

Fiberglass: This is a trade name for a fabric woven from fine filaments of glass. Sometimes used for automobile bodies, it has great strength, and resists heat, chemicals and soil. However, it can be quite soft and pliable.

Flannel: Wool or cotton fabric of coarse soft yarns that are "napped". This means the ends of the yarn are loosened during production of this soft clothing and bedsheet material. You may see it used as an upholstery material.

Frisé: Pronounced "free-zay", this is a pile fabric with uncut loops. It can be produced using most materials and is very durable. You may have seen it on lobby sofas in old movie houses. It is usually produced in nylon for commercial uses, and those old movie-house sofas will probably outlive our society.

Gabardine: A hard-finished twill not often used for upholstery fabrics. It is firm and durable. Your better clothes will often feature this fabric.

Gingham: A lightweight yarn-dyed cotton material, usually woven in checks or stripes. You will often find it at your favorite Italian restaurant—no, not on the menu, under it.

Homespun: A term used to describe hand-loomed woolen textiles. The look can also be produced using power looms.

Khaki: A heavy cotton-twill fabric, traditionally an earth-brown color. The word now describes either the fabric or the color. It was first produced in India as a tough material for English military uniforms. In the 1950s it was worn every day by eastern schoolboys as the pants of choice.

Lace: An openwork textile produced by needle, pin or bobbin, by the process of sewing, knitting, or crocheting. It was first made in Greece, but then spread to most European countries as a cottage industry. Real lace is a handmade product seldom seen in the marketplace because so few craftspeople make it these days. However, lace can also be produced on power looms.

Lampas: A fabric similar to satin damask, it is made of silk, rayon, wool or cotton.

Leno: A type of weave that results in a fabric with a netlike appearance. You will seldom see this weave. I included it because I have hopes that this comment will get me on the Jay Leno Show.

Matelasse: A double or compound fabric with a quilted character and raised patterns that create a puckered or pocketed effect. It is seldom seen on sample furniture in western retail stores. It has more appeal back east and in the south. However, it is generally very expensive and thus not a big player in the current world of upholstery.

Micro-fiber or Microfiber:. Yarn made from polyester that is extremely fine and can be knitted, woven, even flocked to produce a smooth, silky, or even furry hand. Most often used in the furniture industry to produce easily cleaned suede fabrics: i.e., Ultrasuede and Sensuede are the two most common trademarked names for the material.

Mohair: Yarn and cloth made from the fleece of the angora goat. The fiber is wiry and strong, making mohair one of the most durable of all textile fabrics. It had a great surge of popularity during the late 1950s as the sweater material all young ladies had to have.

Moiré: A finish that produces a watermarked appearance on silk or cotton cloth.

Muslin: Plain, woven, white cotton fabric, bleached or unbleached. Its principal use in furniture has been as a base cover on upholstered items before the outer upholstery fabric is added. This double-covering of an upholstery item is seldom done any more, in the interest of reducing the cost of manufacturing. It was a common practice as late as the 1970s with most higher-end manufacturers.

Needlepoint: An old-fashioned cross-stitch done on net, heavy canvas or linen. This is an embroidery technique which, along with lace-making, is seldom done by hand any more. The needlepoint effect can be produced on power looms and is seen on a limited basis in furniture showrooms today.

Nylon: One of the great inventions of the modern world, this material is a wonder of chemistry. It is tough, elastic, and very flexible in its applications. It is often used today in textiles where silk and rayon were the previous fibers of choice.

Paisley: A printed or woven design in imitation of original Scotch shawl patterns made in the town of Paisley, Scotland. This isn't important for most of you, but I always did wonder about those paisley ties I used to buy!

Percale: A plain, closely-woven fabric of muslin in a dull finish which may be bleached, dyed, or printed. It is very similar to chintz.

Plush: Fabric with a long pile, made of silk, wool, cotton or a synthetic fiber. It is made like a velvet and the nap is sometimes pressed down to form a surface resembling fur.

Poplin: A durable, plain-weave class of fabrics made of silk, cotton, wool, synthetics, or any combination of these fibers.

Quilted fabric: A double fabric with padding between the layers held in place by stitching that is usually done in a pattern. It is still a big part of an eastern, southern, or midwestern store's line-up but has limited appeal in the west. Quilting greatly adds to the cost of the fabric. To keep costs in line, a technique called a "combination quilt" is used: The inside areas of the sofa or chair are upholstered with the quilted material, and the outside areas, sides, and back are upholstered using the same fabric but unquilted. A significant cost reduction can be achieved without robbing from the look of the item.

Rayon: Another wonder of the chemical lab, rayon is more lustrous, stiffer, and less expensive than silk. In combination with silk, wool, or cotton, its possibilities are limitless.

Rep: Plain-weave fabric made with a heavy filler thread that gives a corded effect. Rep is unpatterned and reversible, and can be made using any fiber.

Sailcloth: Similar to canvas, it is very durable and often used as a summer-furniture material.

Sateen: A strong, lustrous, cotton fabric with a very smooth surface.

Satin: Smooth, generally lustrous fabric, with a thick, close texture, made of silk. The fibers can be manmade or natural, done in a satin-weave.

Strié: A fabric with a narrow streak or striped effect that is almost the same color as the background. The term "striated" is used to describe the striped effect on any fabric.

Synthetic fibers: Rayon, nylon, bemberg, celanese, dacron, fortisan, lurex, orlon, herculon, all can be used on their own to produce fabrics, or in combination with natural fibers to produce wonderful new looks and hand (feel). Few inventions of modern chemistry have had more impact on modern society than these products.

Taffeta: A fabric woven in basic plain weave, usually made of silk, with warp and weft threads of equal size.

Tapestry: Heavy hand-woven or machine-woven fabric with decorative designs that usually depict historical scenes. The pattern appears on both sides of the fabric with the difference that, on the back side, the loose thread ends are visible. Tapestry works were first used as wall coverings to honor great events of the age, or classical themes. Many tapestries that have survived since they were hand-produced in the seventeenth and eighteenth centuries are true works of art.

Tweed: A class of rough wool fabrics with wiry, somewhat hairy surfaces, but a soft and flexible texture. The weave may be plain, twill, herringbone, or a novelty weave. Generally thought of as a Scottish weave, it is not necessarily limited to Scotland. However, if you are involved in a wager about the source of a tweed, always pick Scotland. You will be right more often than wrong.

Velour: A general term for any fabric that resembles velvet. By the way, velours is the French word for velvet. Remember this if you are ever looking for a velvet sofa in Paris.

Velvet: Fabric having a thick, short pile on the surface and a plain back. It is now usually made by weaving face to face, and then slicing the fabric in two. Velvets can be of all cotton, linen, silk, synthetic, or any combination of the above.

Velveteen: This fabric is woven, and then the loops are sheared to produce the fine close pile. Sometimes called cotton velvet, it is not woven face to face as is velvet.

Vinyl: A textile fused or coated with vinyl plastic. The surface can be printed or embossed. It is most often used in the furniture world as an inexpensive substitute for leather. In combination with leather, it keeps down the price of a chair or sofa without really affecting the look. Don't turn up your nose at this versatile product—it can offer you a nice inexpensive solution to many home decorating problems.

7

....

LEATHER
Its Rich Beauty Comes from Natural Variations!

Leather is a hot seller. I must admit to a real bias when I am talking about leather: I frankly used to believe that you can't buy a good leather sofa for much less than $2,000 or a good leather chair for less than $1,000. This must be my age showing, or the years I spent handling quality leather items, but times have changed and are changing even now as I write these words. In fact with China now getting into the business of producing leather items and shipping them to the American market the World of Leather will never again be the exclusive domain of men's clubs and the wealthy. With the dramatic increase in the use of the new microfibers and their ability to create wonderful suede leather "looks", everyone can now experience the pleasure of "leather" without yesterday's expense.

The largest producers of leather product, with few exceptions, are Italian: Natuzzi (the world's largest leather producer), Chateau d'Ax, Nicoletti, Ital Design, Interline, Flep and Calia. US-based companies include Klaussner (now perhaps as big as Natuzzi), La-Z-Boy, Action, Leather Trend, Thomasville, Leather Center, and Soft Line. In addition, there is Palliser, a Canadian company. These companies represent the lion's share of the leather business, but very close on their heels are producers like Bradington-Young, Hancock & Moore, Drexel-Heritage, Henredon and Roche Bobois—and this group represents what I consider the best manufacturers of quality leather furniture in the country, if not the world. And now a new element has come into the leather world and that is leather upholstery coming out of China. Is it good? It is too early to tell but it sure is priced right!

Italians have shown the world how to do leather inexpensively but with great style. How did they do it? I don't think it is any more complicated than the fact that they took a new look at leather upholstery, found ways in which to cut costs without making the product look cheap, and recognized that there is a huge market for leather items if the cost is kept down and the look is kept up. They did it. Now the question is, should you buy it? Not too long ago I would have said "no", but now the better answer is "maybe". Let's take a look at what leather is all about and see where the best buys are.

Leather is, of course, a natural product. It is the skin of an animal (most often) or reptile (seldom used in upholstered furniture because it would probably take five thousand crocodiles or four thousand snakes to do a sofa) treated to stop the chemical action that would naturally cause it to decay. The treatment or tanning of animal skins goes back thousands of years. What has changed dramatically are the dyes and surface treatments that give leather today's look.

A small aside, but an important one to most consumers today, is the fact that leather, unlike fur, is never a factor in the killing of an animal. The hide of an animal is simply a byproduct of the normal process of producing meat and other animal products for society's needs.

> **SEVEN LIFETIMES**
>
> The furniture industry rates the "wearability" of leather at four to seven times that of fabric.

Since leather is a natural product, subject to all the variables and imperfections possible in any natural product, the word "leather" alone gives you very little information about its quality or how it has been handled. Because the retailer isn't specific when using the word, the consumer must be careful not to assume too much when hearing leather advertised, or mentioned by a salesperson. Leather can be either good or bad, depending on many factors, including: Was the animal healthy to begin with? Was the hide properly processed? What part of the hide is it? How thick is the leather? Compounding the problem for the consumer is the quality level of the sofa or chair frame, as well as the quality of cushions and pillow cores covered in leather.

A quality leather sofa or chair can still be beautiful at twenty or thirty years of age! This is what you want in leather furniture. In order for an item to achieve this age and retain its quality, the frame must have this same "wearability". I am still reluctant to believe that less expensive leather items are going to live up to the anticipated long-term wear and charm that we expect from quality leather upholstery.

Interestingly, the most supple, most lovely, most sexy of leathers are often the most fragile—although tough to wear out, leather is easy to stain or mark, and will fade in strong sunlight. A top grain, aniline-dyed leather, with the hand (feel) of velvet and the color of straw, from a top producer (let's say Hancock and Moore) that just set you back $3,000, can look like an old catcher's mitt in a year. Is there something wrong with the leather?

No. Always keep in mind that, while it is not going to wear out, leather is going to age, to change its character, to change its look. One of the wonders of natural products is that they are constantly changing visually, for better or for worse. Even the fussiest housekeeper cannot keep wonderfully soft aniline-dyed leathers from picking up oils from skin and ink from newspapers, or prevent it wrinkling when someone sits on it. These things are going to happen, so if you want your leather sofa to go on looking like it just came off the showroom floor, watch out for those leathers that are marked pure aniline, naked aniline, naked leather or even semi-aniline. Although you may see these super-soft leathers on less expensive items, these super leathers are generally used by high-end producers, so remember—the cost of an item does not always mean it is going to be the most durable selection you can make. I can guarantee you that the most expensive naked aniline leather sofa, in a family room along with four teenagers, a dog, two cats and a family that likes to entertain, will look like the old fraternity-house-sofa within a year, even though it cost $5,000 or more.

In the room I just described, you should go with pigmented leather and a new supply of Prozac.

SHOPPING FOR LEATHER

Now, when you look through the advertisements in your local newspapers, or walk through your local stores, you see leather sofas advertised from $900 or less, to $6,000 or more. How can that be?

You may see that the producer of the $900 item is touting a lifetime warranty on the frame. You may even see the term "top grain" used to identify the leather. As I have indicated, descriptive terms used in the furniture industry have very fuzzy applications and—since this is an industry with many players and few referees—the only person you can absolutely count on to be well informed is yourself. Keep your eyes open and keep asking those questions that ensure you will buy exactly what you need at a price that reflects the item's true value. There are many ways a low-end manufacturer can reduce the amount it costs him to produce leather upholstered furniture, but he will still advertise the wonders of leather and what it will do for you.

One of my main points in writing this book is to remind you that proper selection of an item consists of more than merely looking at the price and deciding, "If it's expensive it must be good." You can—and will—save yourself a great deal of money by honestly evaluating the ways in which a piece will be used, and then buying accordingly. This is where the Italian breakthrough in less expensive leather upholstery has made a major contribution. The way the Italians shaved the cost of their product is nothing mysterious. American producers could have done the same things, and can still do the same things. Although few of our upper-end producers have elected to compete at the starting price point levels, and have simply let this

---

WHAT IS ANILINE?

Aniline is a family of chemicals from which many dyes are derived. It is quite toxic but you can be sure there is no toxic aniline left in the leather once it reaches its final upholstery application. The advantage of aniline dye is its great clarity.

end of the business go, the largest American producer, Klaussner, competes head-on with the Italians, and could at this moment be the biggest producer of leather upholstery in the world.

How do they all keep the prices down? One of the major ways is to produce a sofa or chair in which leather is used only on the cushions and pillows. The rest of the item will be covered in a color-compatible vinyl. A second method uses leather on all the inside surfaces of an item (top and inside arm, cushion and pillows) and vinyl on all the outside areas (back, outside arms, skirt base). Another cost-saving approach is to use leather "splits" or the middle and bottom layers of a hide that has been sliced top to bottom, then put top grain leather only on cushions and pillows.

A big cost-cutting measure is the use of cheap hides. A cheap hide is available for a number of reasons; one being that it may have been shipped in from a country that often produces less than healthy animals. Without trying to start an international incident, I would suggest many Third World Countries as a source for inexpensive hides. If these hides are not split, however, they could even be called top grain.

Another major cost saving is in the use of split hides as the principal cover. There is nothing dramatically wrong with a split hide—it is still leather, after all. It just doesn't have the beauty or the strength of top grain. There are also less expensive hides available, such as water buffalo, which does not have the look or feel of cowhide. In addition to these methods, there are many ways manufacturers save costs in the tanning process.

Once you get past the cost-cutting tricks involving the leather itself, you come to the frame, springs, and other components of an upholstery frame. Low-end producers have their methods of cutting costs in these areas as well. The bottom line is: You get what you pay for. However, smart shoppers only pay for what they need. This is one of my main points.

I must give lower-end producers credit, however, for making one of life's great luxuries—a leather chair or sofa, often with great style and adequate quality—available to a large number of consumers. Indulge yourself—go out and buy one. Buy two. The industry needs it.

What about the "new" microfibers that look like suede leather?

Fantastic! Actually the "new" microfibers are not new. We all know Ultrasuede and Sensuede. These wonder fabrics have been around for years but mostly as somewhat expensive suede looks. Today the "new" microfibers are the result of new techniques that produce a "thread" that is extremely fine and is being used to produce everything from skivvies to dress slacks. The impact that it is having on the furniture world is that the new microfibers are making the suede look very, very affordable. The microfiber is strong, easy to clean and again very, very affordable. In fact they are so good they look, and when talking about them, like they are too good to be true. For once there is something that is really not too good to be true!

LETTING THE AIR OUT

Why do you see fabric on the bottom of a leather seat cushion? In the old days, producers used small round brass devices on the back boxing of a cushion to release the air trapped when a leather cushion is compressed by someone sitting on it. These small devices cannot release the air very quickly, however, so if you sit down again you may feel as though you're sitting on top of a balloon rather than a cushion. A fabric bottom releases the air almost immediately. If you see fabric on the bottoms of cushions or even the backs of leather pillows, don't be alarmed—and don't think the producers are cutting corners. They aren't. They're letting the air out.

You are going to run into a whole host of proprietary names being used to describe them on furniture floors. Natuzzi uses the term "Dreamfibre". Euroleather uses "Eurosuede". LeatherTrend has decided on "Caress" and Palliser uses "Butterfly". BenchCraft has an exclusive on its cover called "Vera Suede". Are all of these "microfibers" the same? Yes and no. Like any product there is a range of quality that will fall under a common name and microfiber is just another example of your need to ask good questions and to become informed about the many variations that you are going to run into on furniture floors. Talk with your salesperson. Read the literature. Shop around and gather information from many sources and soon you will begin to become comfortable with this new wonder fiber. Bottom-line: This is another example of the "old" giving way to the "new" and making what had been only available to the wealthy now available to everyone. Not bad!

HOW TO CARE FOR LEATHER

As I indicated previously, there is an irony about the care you have to give your leather upholstery. On the one hand, it is the longest-wearing, toughest covering you can put on your upholstered items but, on the other hand, present-day super soft luxurious leathers can be a trial for the owner. When selecting and buying today's leathers it is very important to understand just what kind of housekeeping person you are. If you love the look of an old saddle, or the catcher's mitt in your closet, and think your wallet looks better as it gets older, you may be relaxed enough to buy one of today's super leathers. On the other hand, if you think perfection is a spot-free, blemish-free, consistent color, you had better go for a pigmented leather. Proper selection can—and will—solve most of your leather-care problems and concerns.

The second most important consideration—one that is easily controllable—in the care of your leather items (or fabric items, for that matter) is the personal cleanliness of the person who uses them. Let's face it, if your hobby is changing the oil in your cars every weekend and, immediately after doing so, you come in to watch TV, I wouldn't recommend you buy a pure, aniline-dyed, sand-beige sofa. You could go with a wonderful London glazed tufted sofa in a deep burgundy leather and end up being as happy as the proverbial clam. Choose properly at the beginning, and half your troubles will go away.

Let's say you have chosen properly and the item is in your home—what do you do now? Actually, present-day leathers need very little care. Almost every furniture store sells leather-cleaning kits that are a great help in keeping your leather upholstery in good shape. "The Guardsman Leather Care Kit" is my favorite. "Leather Master" also has a good care package. You will find several leather care kits in good hardware stores and even in well stocked grocery stores; but don't forget that the first step is keeping your items as dust-free as possible. Vacuum often and occasionally wipe the arms and the top of the back (where your head touches) with a soft cloth dampened in a mild detergent solution. This will cut through any oil buildup from your hands or hair. Always try very hard to keep leather furniture out of direct sunlight, because sunlight is guaranteed to fade anything, except you. Every six months or so I get my leather-care kit out and, by following the directions carefully, give my leather items a going-over. But before you do the same, make sure you know what kind of leather you have. Each piece must be cleaned according to the type of leather used in it. You will not clean nubuck in the same way you clean a heavily pigmented glazed leather. Pay attention and, when in doubt, have a professional do it. And never use saddle soap on your leather upholstery.

LEATHER GLOSSARY

Here are some of the key terms you will hear when shopping for leather.

Aniline: A transparent dye used to color leather all the way through. It is considered transparent because it doesn't cover or conceal range marks or any natural graining of the leather.

Pure aniline: Somewhat redundant, it is a term often used to denote an unprotected aniline-dyed leather. It should mean "watch out" if you cannot stand to see an item of furniture change and develop character—that means it is getting marked up.

Semi-aniline: Also called aniline-plus or protected aniline. Top-grain leather aniline-dyed and coated with matching pigment (color) to even out the over-all color and provide some protection.

Antique/distressed: These terms apply any time a leather has been given marks to simulate natural aging and wear. These terms also apply to wood furniture treated to create aged looks.

Corrected grain: Leather buffed to remove undesirable blemishes and embossed (a pattern pressed under pressure into the leather) to simulate an attractive grain (like crocodile) or other decorative texture.

Full grain: Top-grain leather with no corrections or alterations to the natural grain pattern. Not often seen except at the very high end. This term is used in Europe interchangeably with "top grain".

Leather-vinyl combination: The use of leather with matching vinyl on the sides and back of a sofa or chair. Cost saving measure which, when done well, looks quite good.

Natural markings or range marks: Common marks on leather, which occurred when the animal was doing its thing on the range: Barbed-wire marks, healed scratches, wrinkles, insect bites, stretch marks—all of these marks can be simulated today.

Nubuck: Top-grain, aniline-dyed leather buffed to create a soft nap, very vulnerable to stains, so it is often lightly finished to offer some protection. Usually quite expensive, nubuck can look like a suede but it isn't. Suede is made from a split hide, thus not as fine a piece of leather as nubuck.

Patina: Describes that luster or shine that develops with use over time. This term is often used for the wonderful glow fine old wood furniture and other antiques acquire over the years. Fussy customers work hard for the clean look that only plastic will deliver every day. Relax, use your fine things—care for them, but use them, and years from now someone will remark on the wonderful patina an item of yours has acquired.

Pigmented leather: Finished with a solid-pigment coating to achieve consistent color and texture, the opposite of dyed leather. Dye gives a clear look at the leather grain, pigment does not. You might say dye is similar to stain and pigment is similar to paint. This style of finish goes back quite a way and is characterized initially by a high-gloss look. As pigmented leather is used, and flexes under the pressure of sitting, it gradually develops tiny surface cracks in the finish. You'll have noticed such tiny cracks every time you sat in Grandpa's chair. Could be your best choice in high-traffic situations, for tough wear and a measure of invulnerability to spills and other everyday use.

Pull-up: Full grain, aniline-dyed leather, waxed or oiled. It will have a somewhat oily hand (feel) that has a richness to it. I often think of it as having life to it as opposed to the more routine leathers. Generally found at the upper end of the leather market.

Sauvage: A visual effect that produces a mottled, or tone-on-tone look, a technique used to add character or depth to a leather.

Split: The bottom layers of the hide that have been split off from the top grain. Pigmented or made into a suede, one of the big cost-saving devices utilized by lower-end producers.

Suede: See nubuck. See also split. See my comments on microfibers.

Top coat: Transparent protective coating applied to leather surface.

Top grain: This is the best: The uppermost layer of the hide. This is what you want—this is one of the hallmarks of a quality item, particularly if the whole item is covered in top grain.

8

PERSONAL STYLE

Of Recliners and Designers, and How to Get the Best from Each

Remember when recliners were the size of small refrigerators but not as good-looking? In those days if you were working with an interior decorator or designer, and you wanted a recliner, you would have been in for an argument. Happily, today's recliners can be beautiful, and what's more, a decorator's attitude toward your favorite recliner is one quick way to learn whether this is a person you can work with, and whose work you can live with.

THE UGLY DUCKLING THAT BECAME A SWAN

Not only can today's motion furniture be beautiful, it can also work better than the original recliners. Gone, for the most part, is the crank on the side to facilitate the reclining action. Gone is the tremendous bulk needed to handle the reclining mechanism. Gone is the idea that motion itself justifies almost any degree of ugly. Gone (almost) is the designer's reluctance to use a recliner in a room plan.

These days, you should have one or two recliners. They can be wonderful. The recliner of the nineties is essentially a chair or sofa that has been fitted with a reclining mechanism. The information we have already covered concerning quality features in stationary furniture also applies to motion furniture. The only new element is the improved reclining mechanism.

Recliners now range from elegant to high tech, with everything from massage units to speaker telephones, holders for your beverage and places for your magazines, but—to my mind—the most important new element is the fact that present-day recliners can fit into the most tastefully decorated room because there is such a broad range of styles available.

THE BEST OF THE RECLINERS
Bradington-Young
Hancock & Moore

THE GOOD RECLINERS
La-Z-Boy
Barcalounger

THE BASIC RECLINERS
Action
Benchcraft
Berkline
Catnapper
Strato-lounger

Think about motion furniture the next time you need a comfortable chair or sofa for your home. It can be a real treat after a long, hard day. And, if any of you have hired designers or decorators who would never consider using a recliner in a room, just fire them!

SHOULD YOU USE AN INTERIOR DESIGNER OR DECORATOR?

This question has so many ramifications that a simple "yes" or "no" just will not suffice. The long answer includes the word "depends". The answer depends upon the abilities of the designer or decorator in question.

To begin with, the terms "designer" and "decorator" should mean different things. There really is a significant difference between the two, but in the present marketplace they are often used interchangeably. A designer should be someone who can take an empty space and both design it and decorate it. A decorator is an individual who simply takes a planned space and puts items into it. It seems like a minor point to most consumers, however, in the trade, a qualified designer is (and should be) insulted when referred to as a mere decorator. Designers are more than that, and if they have the training and experience, they deserve the term "interior designer".

What makes this field hard to investigate is the fact that almost anyone can claim to be a designer or decorator. There is no agency in government or industry to police this field. You, the consumer, are really on your own. There are, however, professional organizations. The American Society of Interior Designers (ASID) has rigid high standards to be met before anyone can use the ASID designation. The Interior Design Society (IDS) has professional standards which, while not as demanding as the those of the ASID, do tell you that you are dealing with someone who is far more than a design "wannabe".

In the early 1990s, California tried to introduce a stiff state examination for certification of all interior designers in the state. Anyone who passed would then be "State Certified" and allowed to claim the designation CCID, but in the present world of diluted standards it simply isn't enforceable. Thus, consumers are left with the responsibility of determining who is qualified to give advice about making a home beautiful. The bottom line for you is this: If the person you are hiring presents proof of ASID or IDS membership, or CCID qualification (in California) or a combination of the above, you will know that individual is equipped with some academic and/or professional experience in the practice of interior design.

Does that solve all your problems? Absolutely not. The most academically- or professionally-prepared person may not be good for you if the two of you do not communicate well with one another. This statement almost sounds trite, but communication is critical if you want your space to be right for you and for your lifestyle. Only you know what will work for you in terms of budget, color and scale. Only you know what you want your space to say about you—everything we wear, own, say, join, and read makes a statement about us, so we are always, in some way, making personal statements, to ourselves and to those around us.

The designers and decorators you select must be clever enough and professional enough to really hear what you are saying if they have any hope of pleasing you.

In a very real sense, the best designer for you is you, but often you lack the time and tools to do the job properly. This is why we turn to the experts. We know what we want but we also know that, to achieve that extra panache, that extra touch, that magic, we may need the experienced expert. A good designer will help put the magic in your home.

There are a few key points to help you recognize an experienced designer or decorator. The first and most important is the ability to listen. The client tells the designer what to do—not the other way around. Therefore, the designer must find out what styles the client likes and what the client's lifestyle is, taking into account whether there are children or pets in the house and other variables. The designer must also determine who has the major input in the project (husband? wife? both?) and, most of all, what the client wants to accomplish. These points should all be established before any major design project is undertaken.

Many furniture retailers offer an interior design service on a no-charge basis when merchandise is bought from their store. They may also have design staff who work at an hourly rate on projects that do not necessarily involve purchases. In addition, there are numerous independent designers who charge an hourly rate to help you select furniture locally or take you to one of the metropolitan design centers. Usually, designers receive a professional discount at design showrooms, which they may or may not pass along to the customer. You should also be aware that not all furniture brands are available to independent designers—or to retail furniture stores, for that matter. In addition, buying through one of the large metropolitan design centers is not necessarily an avenue to great savings.

THANK GOODNESS FOR MARTHA STEWART, ALEXANDRA STODDARD AND ILSE CRAWFORD

These three ladies—there are others, but these three, celebrities and prolific writers all—best represent the celebration of the home that we now see in magazines and books, as well as on television. Over the years the design trade has celebrated the home, but it was usually the elitist home. It was the home of big money. It was the home on the hill. It was the home that most of us didn't have. The message was loud and clear: If you have money, your home will be magnificent. If you don't have money—well, make sure you give us the privacy to enjoy our big homes and, while you're at it, keep working so that maybe some day you too can live like this.

Listen to the message in the following quotation from a major interior design book written for working designers: "Many designers frown on the use of reproductions, regarding them as a form of fakery that is dishonest when it truly deceives, foolish when it fails to deceive. Designer and client must judge this issue according to a particular context. For example, reproduction captain's chairs in a restaurant designed in a particular style may seem easier to accept than a brand new imitation Chippendale breakfront in a living room!"

Give me a break! (Incidentally, it serves no purpose for me to identify the writer of that statement. I have the information, if anyone is interested, but the individual really isn't important—this is an example of the arrogance of many in the design trade when they come into contact with the great unwashed public.)

So we went on our way collectively thinking that wonderful homes were beyond our ken. But then along came the Three Musketeers of the Home, who told us what we should have known all along: It doesn't take money and a hilltop to make a home magnificent. What it takes is an aware man and woman who celebrate their home each day, filling it with the warm smells of life until the home becomes magnificent (even if the breakfront in the living room is a Chippendale reproduction bought at The Furniture Barn for $1,200).

ECLECTIC, RETRO, AND COUNTRY

Do we have three country music groups here? No. What we have are the buzz words you will hear when you shop for furniture in the near future. Buzz words change all the time but, interestingly, some can hang around for quite a while. Eclectic is one such term, and you will often hear it from designers and decorators to describe a mix of styles in a room. A French Country armoire with a fine English Manor commode, perhaps with a wonderful brass bed and, let's say, a pair of Oriental black lacquer night stands. This would be an eclectic mix of styles all coming together with the use of color and accessories to create an exciting "collected" look. Many people feel best surrounded by an exciting mix of individually important items that have very little to do with their companions. It doesn't matter that the finishes are different or the hardware doesn't match. It doesn't matter that one item has a curved leg and the other a straight leg. What matters is that each piece is wonderful in its own right. Once you have selected or acquired the items, you then pull the room together with your fabric selections, your lighting and your accessories.

This is the way I like my rooms to look. I always have a place for a wonderful piece of furniture no matter what style it is. Would this approach be right for you? Only if you can be comfortable with this much variation. Many people want eighteenth-century cherry from the front door to the back door, and this is right—for them. You must remember what I have said all along: Do what pleases you and you will be pleased. Does this mean we always know what will please us? Absolutely not, and this is why we shop. This is why we browse through magazines. This is why we travel. This is why we learn. We do all of these things in order to broaden our knowledge, to give us perspective, and to give us depth.

Taste is a function of appreciation, while style is a function of security. We can improve our taste levels by investigating everything offered in this world but, until we are secure within ourselves, we can never develop a style that is unique. Our style then becomes the benchmark with which we choose objects for our surroundings. You will know what is right for you. You will feel it in your bones. Whatever it is, from 1750s country to 1950s retro or the most modern statement, you will find it in the stores of your cities and towns. If you don't see what you want, don't buy anything. Don't compromise with something that is almost right. Wait for the right pieces. You will find them—and the joy of discovery, you will find, is half the fun. Good hunting!

9

....

THE STORE IS NOT THE ENEMY!
Preparation Is the Key

We all have to learn how to relax when we walk into a furniture store. The store isn't the enemy until we make it so and so often our attitudes make our search for best buys and best merchandise almost impossible to achieve. Why? Well I'll tell you. I have been watching the opening scenario at furniture stores for almost fifty years now. A consumer walks through the front door and is greeted by a receptionist or floor person almost immediately; and if you are not greeted immediately you are either in a poorly run store or one that has very few personnel. What do you do? Well if you are like most people you will say, "No I don't need any help I am just looking". So you stroll around the store and look at a few prices sit in a chair or sofa; perhaps go to the bathroom, and then you turn around and leave. Heaven's but that is not the way to gather information or to gain any real appreciation as to what the store is all about. We all do it. I even do it still and kick myself every time. In all fairness to ourselves I think part of our reluctance to be more aggressive, no that isn't the word, perhaps assertive, is the feeling that we don't want to spend some salesperson's time if we are not ready to buy. Please stop thinking this way. I don't know any furniture storeowner who wouldn't beg you to stop and question a salesperson and find out everything you want to know about the store and the merchandise the store carries. Why not? How else are you going to find out if you and your pocket book fit the store and how else is the store personnel going to do their best to make you their client?

What if you don't see the sofa, or chair, or whatever that you are carrying around in your mind? You must stop and ask questions. A good salesperson/designer/decorator has a wealth of knowledge that he or she wants to share with you. Of course they want you to buy something; but the very best ones know that you will end-up buying something from them if they connect with you. The burden is on them. Not you. You may need to go into several stores before you begin to feel that one particular store is right for you. Most important don't think any one store can fill all your needs. There is simply too much furniture product available for any one store or any chain of stores to get their hands around all of it.

Think of the store as a resource that you can use to make the most of your plan to furnish your home. But to accomplish your plan you must communicate completely with everyone who can help you bring it all together. What I just said is often a bone of contention with store owners and store designers. Why? Because they often are reluctant to share their time and knowledge with a shopper who they suspect will be picking their brain for ideas and then will leave and call an 800 number in North Carolina to order the furniture that they helped you decide on. Does it happen? Absolutely. All the time if you listen to a storeowner talk. I personally think it happens too often but I don't think it happens as often as the average store owner or designer thinks it does. Would you do it? Would you take advantage of a store's personnel and then turn around an use their work when ordering the product that they helped you select if I gave you an 800 number to call in North Carolina? Most consumers would not. Some consumers will do it in a heartbeat. I hope you won't. I have found over the years that the best-designed and best-decorated homes are those homes that result from a close collaboration between a very good designer and a very committed homeowner consumer. The homes that are filled with product bought by someone chasing a discount look just that way. Uncoordinated. Uninspired. Undone.

So what should you do if everyone in the retail game is suspicious, cautious, reluctant to share, uninformed, fearful, etc.? By George it sounds like the plot of a bad movie and in a way it is. Why it is bad is simply the fact that too often the main players are at cross-purposes. If the store isn't receptive, ready, and sharp for you when you enter the front door and you are not receptive, ready, and sharp when it comes to your preparation then you can see what a disappointment most furniture shopping events can be. The results of all this confusion and lack of preparation results in money wasted and opportunities lost both for you as a consumer and for the store as a merchant.

It doesn't have to be this way. Let me tell you how to approach any store and any store's personnel. Relax, Smile, Preparation and Communication are the keys to a successful venture into any store. Remember you will not be wasting their time. What you want to avoid is wasting your time. Relax about the process. No one is going to sell you anything that you don't say yes to. Just because you don't see what you think you want to buy doesn't mean it isn't available. Most consumers waste time and money because you are and they are in too big of a hurry to make a purchase. Why is it so critical from a time standpoint to want your room or rooms to be filled with furniture over the weekend? Trust me. The faster you run from store to store the less appealing and less satisfying your final result will be. So relax!

OK now that you are relaxed and have smiled at everyone in sight you are ready to start getting the facts. You are ready aren't you? OK you aren't ready. This is perhaps the biggest mistake most furniture shoppers make. They know they want a sofa or what-have-you and they simply go out and look for one in a color they like. Wrong! Wrong! Wrong! You must have a plan. A real plan. At least have it written down on the back of an envelop but it would be better if you have a sketch of the room or rooms that you are looking to develop. You must have your dimensions not only of the room itself but also where the windows are located. The space dimensions of each separate area that you need to concern yourself with. Where is the fireplace and how much room is there beside the fireplace to each wall? Where are the electrical plugs located? Do you have electrical outlets in the floor or do you have to consider running extension cords, etc.? What kind of traffic flow will the room experience? How much seating do you need in the room? Does the room need to be painted? What about your window treatments? Should they be changed? What do you see when you look through the window? Should you have a more attractive view when you look out? Perhaps a new bush or a new artifact. What about the floor covering? Should you change it? In short, never think of a furniture purchase as an isolated event. Perhaps you don't need to even buy something new? Simply rearranging what you have, coupled with new paint and new accessories, could do the trick! Unless you have a plan, a real plan, you could be throwing good money away and what is more often the case, you could be buying a new problem to replace an old problem. Bottom-line: the better your planning the happier you will be and the better your rooms will look, not to mention that you will probably spend less money than you thought you would.

Pogo said: "We have seen the enemy and it is us." The biggest problem we have when we are shopping for furniture is the frustration we experienced because we are simply not prepared either in the practical matter of space planning and, of course, when it comes to fundamental knowledge about furniture and home furnishings items. You bought my book and that is a good first step. Now take the next best step and use the store and the store's personnel in the best possible way. They want to help you make a good decision. Let them. Finally be prepared when it comes to your needs and desires to be able to communicate exactly what you want to achieve. Remember the store is not the enemy. Don't you be the enemy. Be prepared and you will be pleased with the results.

10

BRANDS AND STORES

Here's Where to Shop for Furniture, Wherever You Live

Quality rating of manufacturers can only be done if we compare similar manufacturers with one another. It is neither productive nor valid to rate a producer of expensive reproduction furniture with a producer of mass-market furniture. They clearly are not trying to do the same thing. To say one is excellent and the other is poor is to miss the point. Therefore, I compiled a list of furniture manufacturers in alphabetical order, rather than order of quality, then compared each producer's product with the line most similar to it.

I have insisted throughout this book that you judge the value of any product by its cost to you and the benefits it brings you. With this in mind, you can see why I would have Baker furniture in my dining room and Bassett furniture in my son's room, and feel that I have the perfect mix of value and benefits. The following are the brands you will see most often in furniture stores, department stores, and large furniture chain stores across the United States.

BRAND-NAME FURNITURE IN YOUR LOCAL FURNITURE STORES

American Drew: Competes with Bassett. A modest line found in many major stores.

Baker Furniture Company: One of the best. At the very least, one of the top five producers of fine wood and upholstered furniture in the United States. Very expensive, but worth every dollar. Collectable, and surely one of tomorrow's heirlooms.

Bassett Furniture Company: Modest but honest value. Good starter furniture or perfect for kids' rooms and vacation homes. One of the largest domestic producers of casegoods and upholstery.

Bernhardt Furniture Company: A wonderful line of impressive fine wood product. Their approach to finishes has always baffled me a bit as it seems they work hard to produce muted, opaque finishes while I prefer clearer, transparent finishes—a minor point when the line is considered in toto. Absolutely one of the better lines in the United States.

Broyhill Furniture Company: Good values, a well-priced, nicely-styled line. Don't hesitate to give it a good look. Carried by many large chains.

Century Furniture Company: Certainly one of the top ten producers of fine wood furniture and upholstery in the US. Beautifully styled and beautifully finished, a line to look for when considering the best.

Drexel-Heritage Furniture Company Its best collections are as good as it gets. A big lineup of product from modest to expensive. I always consider Drexel the point where price and value meet. Pay more and you get more glitter, but not more value. Pay less and you really are getting less. The Heritage product is as good as it gets. Heritage competes directly with Century and Henredon.

Ethan Allen Furniture Company: One of the great success stories in the furniture world. Its product assortment and store presentations have set the standard for all other producers to follow. You will never be unhappy with an Ethan Allen purchase. Generally priced at the lower end of the Drexel and Thomasville lines.

Ferguson Copeland: A newer company that is offering a tremendous amount of style and pizzaz for the money. Check them out.

Flexsteel Furniture Company: One of the country's largest producers of upholstery product. Good, solid, reliable upholstery, well-priced and well-styled.

Hancock & Moore: Excellent leather furniture. Generally considered to be the top of the line for leather upholstery.

Hekman Furniture Co.: Upper-end company manufacturing mostly occasional furniture. They have an excellent desk program. Good quality. Priced near Drexel and Thomasville.

Henredon Furniture Company: One of the top ten producers of fine wood and upholstered furniture. Beautiful finishes, beautiful woodwork, beautiful design. If you own Henredon, you own some of the very best.

Highland House Furniture Co.: One of the country's top producers of fine upholstery. Beautiful designs, careful, excellent quality standards. You will never make a mistake buying this product.

Hooker Furniture Company: Medium-priced entertainment centers, bedroom and occasional furniture. Excellent value. One of the leading producers of entertainment centers. A good buy. Give them a good look.

Lane Furniture Company: Middle of the road. Competes with Lexington and below.

Lexington Furniture Company: One of the great values in wood furniture in the United States. I believe Lexington gives you more bang for your buck than any other line in the country. Is it the best? No, but it may be the best value. Lexington is a consistent industry leader in style offerings.

Maitland-Smith Furniture Company: One of the largest and earliest developers of exciting wood product coming out of the Philippines. Many unusual pieces, a very exciting line. Heavy in occasional wood furniture. Uses techniques that cannot be touched by mainland producers. Even with all the excitement and style, a very affordable collection of items. Very influential in the industry.

Natuzzi Furniture Company: One of the world's biggest producers of leather upholstery. Perhaps some of the best-styled leather product to be found anywhere. I don't think it is the best quality but, for the money, you may not be able to do better.

Pennsylvania House Furniture Company: A consistent producer of good traditional wood furniture and upholstery. Long in the shadow of Ethan Allen, it deserves its own place in the sun. It would be a mistake to miss shopping this fine company.

Pulaski: Competes with Stanley but usually a little more dramatic in its presentation.

Stanley Furniture Company: Modestly-priced, often very excitingly-styled furniture. Excellent value, a good line for your first home. Usually priced below Lexington.

Sumter Cabinet: Well-priced, solid wood line. Well put-together, although most designs are pretty basic. Very good value.

Thomasville Home Furnishings: A big, well-done line of excellent wood and upholstery. You should always make it a point to shop a Thomasville showcase store. They miss very few bases. A direct competitor with Drexel, Ethan Allen and the upper end of Lexington.

Universal Furniture Company: A big offshore producer of modestly-priced wood furniture. Style and detailing is amazing when you consider their prices. A great value. At or below Stanley.

Vaughan-Bassett: Modest casegoods aimed at the mass marketer. Competes with Bassett and Universal.

SMALLER BRANDS WORTH LOOKING FOR!

Here is another group of manufacturers who, in my opinion, are outstanding but, as smaller producers, often harder to find in many markets. If you see their product in your travels, you will be doing yourself a favor by carefully considering them for your home.

E. J. Victor: Relatively new, but immediately a leading contender for inclusion in our top ten producers of the very finest wood product and upholstery product. Simply magnificent furniture. You will only find it displayed in your area's finest stores. Expensive, but well worth it.

Guy-Chaddock & Company: My personal favorite for the finest country wood pieces produced in the United States. Their finishes are works of art. Even though I said earlier that it couldn't be done, I will say that a piece of Guy-Chaddock can make a room. I would buy a piece from any of their collections, sight unseen, and know I would love it.

Harden Furniture Company: Very good product. Harden offers bedroom, dining and occasional furniture. A small company with good attention to quality. Priced at about Drexel.

Hinckle Harris: Very high quality, solid wood furniture. Many traditional designs. Priced near the top.

Karges Furniture Co.: Expensive and lush. Magnificent wood furniture. Perhaps the most opulent of the American manufacturers. Collectable. Very distinctive design and execution.

Kindel Furniture Company: Kindel's big problem is the ever-diminishing number of purists who appreciate the understated elegance and refinement of this grand line. Expensive, but a true collectible.

Marge Carson Furniture Co.: Distinctive and outstanding producer of fine contemporary wood and upholstered furniture. Some of the most pleasing contemporary designs produced in the US come out of this company. Beautiful finishes that few other producers even attempt. If you are after a look for today and can indulge yourself, you must take a look at Marge Carson. This producer has had a heavy impact on upper-end furniture styles in the US. Priced at the Henredon/Heritage level.

Stickley Furniture Company: The prime mover behind the Arts and Crafts movement and still the force behind the Mission style that is very big now. Stickley is what fine furniture-making is all about. Uncompromising quality and unquestioned status as one of the country's finest wood furniture producers. Expensive, but you will be glad to own a piece of Stickley.

So many other manufacturers could be mentioned, as there are literally hundreds out there in the marketplace. However, I have limited myself to lines you will most likely see as you shop for furniture in your local stores.

THE TOP 100 FURNITURE STORES IN THE UNITED STATES

These stores are ranked by dollar volume. Does this make them the best? No, but it sure does mean that an awful lot of people thought they were good places to buy furniture. Maybe you should give them a look. This ranking is reprinted with permission from the May 26, 2003 issue of **Furniture Today,** the weekly business newspaper of the furniture industry. The location shown is the home base of each company.

1. Rooms To Go, Seffner, Fla.
2. Pier One Imports, Fort Worth, TX.
3. Ethan Allen, Danbury, Conn.
4. Levitz Home Furnishings, Woodbury, N.Y.
5. La-Z-Boy Furniture Galleries, Monroe, Mich.
6. Berkshire Hathaway (furniture division), Omaha, Neb
   See notes at end of section
7. Ikea, Plymouth Meeting, Pa.
8. Havertys, Atlanta, Ga.
9. Value City Furniture, Columbus, Oh.
10. Art Van, Warren, Mich.
11. Rhodes, Atlanta, GA,
12. Thomasville Home Furnishings Stores, Thomasville, N.C.
13. The Bombay Company, Fort Worth, TX.
14. W.S. Badcock, Mulberry, Fla.
15. Pottery Barn, San Francisco, Ca.
16. Raymour & Flanigan, Liverpool, N.Y.
17. Crate & Barrel, Northbrook, Ill.
18. Wickes Furniture, Wheeling, Ill.
19. Breuners Home Furnishings Corp., Lancaster, Pa.
20. Ashley Home Stores, Arcadia, Wis.

21. The Room Store, Richmond, VA.
22. Select Comfort, Minneapolis, Minn.
23. Bassett Furniture Direct, Bassett, VA.
24. American Furniture Warehouse, Englewood, Colo.
25. Slumberland, Little Canada, Minn.
26. Restoration Hardware, Corte Madera, Ca.
27. The Mattress Firm, Houston, TX.
28. Sleepy's, Bethpage, N.Y.
29. Cost Plus, Oakland, Ca.
30. Finger Furniture, Houston, TX.
31. Mattress Discounters, Upper Marlboro, Md.
32. City Furniture, Tamarac, Fla.
33. Robb & Stucky, Fort Meyers, Fla.
34. Mathis Bros., Oklahoma City, Ok.
35. Mattress Giant, Addison, TX.
36. Boyles Furniture, Hickory, N.C.
37. Sofa Express, Groveport, Oh.
38. Furnitureland South, High Point, N.C.
39. ABC Carpet & Home, New York, N.Y.
40. Kane's Furniture, Pinellas Park, Fla.
41. Jennifer Convertibles, Woodbury, N.Y.
42. Bob's Discount Furniture, Manchester, Conn.
43. HOM Furniture, Coon Rapids, Minn.
44. Haynes Furniture, Virginia Beach, VA.
45. Harlem Furniture, Lombard, Ill.
46. El Dorado Furniture, Miami Gardens, Fla.
47. Gallery Furniture, Houston, TX.
48. Rockaway Bedding, Randolph, N.J.
49. Drexel Heritage Home Inspirations, High Point, N.C.
50. Super Stores of America, San Diego, Ca.
51. Carls, Boca Raton, Fla.
52. Baer's, Pompano Beach, Fla.

53. Storehouse, Atlanta, Ga.
54. Norwalk - The Furniture Idea, Norwalk, Oh.
55. Farmers Furniture, Dublin, Ga.
56. Levin Furniture, Smithtown, Pa.
57. Kittles, Indianapolis, Ind.
58. Grand Home Furnishings, Roanoke, VA.
59. Jeromes, San Diego, Ca.
60. The RoomStore, Phoenix, AZ.
61. Leath/Modernage, Atlanta, Ga.
62. Benchmark Home Furnishings, Olathe, Kan.
63. Rose Furniture, High Point, N.C.
64. Homestead House, Broomfield, Colo.
65. Room & Board, Minneapolis, Minn.
66. American Home, Albuquerque, N.M.
67. The Sleep Train, North Highlands, Ca.
68. Lack's, Victoria, TX.
69. Gabberts, Edina, Minn.
70. Dial-A-Mattress, Long Island City, N.Y.
71. Schewel Furniture, Lynchburg, VA.
72. Steinhafels, New Berlin, Wis.
73. Walter E. Smithe Furniture, Itasca, Ill.
74. Bernie & Phyl's, Norton, Mass.
75. Stickley, Audi & Co., Manlius, N.Y.
76. Z Gallerie, Gardena, Ca.
77. Marlo Furniture, Rockville, Md.
78. Wood-Armfield/Utility Craft, High Point, N.C.
79. Domain, Norwood, Mass.
80. Darvin Furniture, Orland Park, Ill.
81. South Dakota Furniture Mart, Sioux Falls, S.D.
82. Big Lots Furniture, Columbus, Oh.
83. Lack's Valley Stores, Pharr, TX.
84. C.S.Wo & Sons, Honolulu, HI.

85. Gardner White, Warren, Mich.

86. Louis Shanks of Texas, Austin, TX.

87. USA Baby, Elmhurst, Ill.

88. Sit'n Sleep, Carson, Ca.,

89. Hank's Fine Furniture, Sherwood, Ark.

90. Kirschman's, New Orleans, La.

91. McMahan's, Los Angles, Ca.

92. Big Sandy Superstores, Franklin Furnace, Oh.

93. Sleep Fair/Mattress Warehouse, Akron, Oh.

94. Wolf Furniture, Bellwood, Pa.

95. Green Front Furniture, Farmville, VA.

96. America Group, Vancouver, WA.

97. Roche-Bobois USA, New York, N.Y.

98. Bay Furniture, Homewood, Ill.

99. Sam Levitz Furniture, Tucson, AZ.

100. Mastercraft Interiors, Beltsville, Md.

There you have the Top 100 Stores in the United States as ranked by their volume. Now it is important for me to state that this ranking does not take into consideration any department stores which are generally considered as a group apart by furniture industry analysts. Macy's, Bloomindales, Dillard's, Sears, and Penney's are representative of many department stores that have significant furniture departments that should be on your list of places to consider when you are beginning your furniture shopping. I said earlier that the ranking does not necessarily mean anything beyond the simple fact that they do a lot of business. Now this simple fact of their doing a lot of business does give you an important benefit as a consumer. Almost without exception each of these stores will display a lot of product for you to consider. In all fairness their large volumes also indicate that a good number of consumers have found the stores to be a good place to shop. At the very least when you are in proximity to any one of these stores you should stop in and see what they have to offer you.

THE BEST STORE IN THE UNITED STATES!

The best store in the country is the Design Galleria by Valentine in Sacramento, CA! I just made 5000 furniture storeowners see red and some of them were friends of mine. Come on now! How can a "smallish" store in a "smallish" market be the

Best Store in the United States? Well let me tell you what I think the "Best Store" has got to be and then you can decide for yourself.

To begin with there are two kinds of furniture stores. One is the store that sells items: sofas, chairs, tables, bedrooms, lamps, and all the other items that go into a home. These kinds of stores are in every town and city in the United States. They can be big stores, and often are, or they can be "mini stores" or furniture departments in large general merchandise stores, or they can be the furniture store on the corner or in the shopping center in your hometown. You stop in and look around trying to find the perfect sofa or chair, or lamp for your home. You see it, or you don't, and you buy it, or you walk out and look for another place to shop. This sequence of events happens every day in every town in the country. These kinds of stores are often staffed by eager, pleasant people who will be very helpful in trying to help you find the item in the store that you are seeking for your home. Many of these stores will have interior decorators, or better yet, interior designers who will try and help you make your selections. Many of these stores are attractively displayed and have a wonderful looking building designed to bring the maximum amount of display available for your consideration. Often these item stores will present a discount approach to all the items they display: 50% off or 30% off tags will be spread throughout the store and their advertising approach will be just that: Buy Now at Massive Savings....2 Years to Pay, No Interest, Terms, and so on. Hey, what's wrong with all that? Absolutely nothing. It is and has been the shape of furniture retailing for the past 50 years or so. It works. Oh furniture stores come and go; but in general, most of us know these stores and have shopped in these stores for years. American Homes are filled with the furniture items that these stores sell. Items, items everywhere and rarely any that add up to a coordinated whole. The average American Home is the envy of the world. The average American lives in better homes with better home furnishings that most of the world's citizens; but our homes could be better and this observation brings us to the 2nd type of furniture store. The store that sells home environments and not just home furnishing items.

Am I splitting hairs here? Yes and No. The 2nd type of furniture store that I am talking about can look just like the Item oriented furniture store that I just described. The environmental oriented store can be big or small. It can be a small free standing independent all the way to a large, multi-state furniture emporium. It will, in all likelihood, look and feel like every well-done furniture store that you have ever been in. The key point is that the "store" will generally present itself to the public in a different way and the sales staff will try very hard to help you develop a plan for your room or rooms (whether you like it or not). Let's face it; a good many consumers do not want the total experience that the environmental oriented store tries to incorporate in each opportunity they have with a consumer. They should; but they often don't. I place the reluctance to the inherent fear that most consumers have of being "sold something" by a salesperson. I hope you try very hard to get over this reluctance to be open with knowledgeable staff and just see what happens. Remember a very important part of any shopping experience is not only to find product but also to get educated as to all the options that are available to you. The store is not the enemy. Keep that in mind. Going on; it will not be a discount-oriented store. It's advertising will be more subdued and will emphasize style and glamour rather than finance terms and "no interest deals". It will be more heavily displayed with accessory items and the merchandise shown in its vignettes will generally be more expensive. Heavens—this is exactly the kind of store you want to stay out of I'll bet! Wrong. This is the kind of store you want to discover and it is these kinds of stores in the U.S. that can help you best to save money, get more value, and have a better looking home. Impossible you say! Let me tell you why and let me share why I said that the Design Galleria by Valentine in Sacramento, Ca. is the "best store" in the country, and why you should try and discover what the "Best Store" in your city and town is.

The biggest difference between the Item Oriented store and the Environmental Oriented store is the attitude of the owner or owners of the store and how this attitude is expressed in the Mission Statement that controls how they are going to run their business. Now the value differences between the Item Oriented store does not make this type of store better or worse than the Environmental Oriented store. All Item Stores are not bad and all Environmentally Oriented stores are not good. What is the mission statement that I mentioned above? The Mission Statement is that informal—but better formally written down—expression of how the owners intend to run their business and how they want to serve their customer clients. Now it is important to realize that there is no wrong attitude as opposed to some mythical right attitude. What the store ownership attitudes are have no moral significance at all. What the store ownership attitudes and business plans do though is permeate down throughout the whole organization and eventually to you the consumer. This is where the big differences between the two types of store come into play and affect you the consumer. The Item Store is just that; it waits for you to buy the sofa, chair, or lamp that you see and take it home. In a nutshell, that is about all there is to shopping in an Item driven store and this is what most furniture stores in the country are like. Hey, consumers get what they want. We created this store and it serves very well for a great number of consumers. But it has always been my contention that many consumers want more: they just can't articulate what "more" they want.

This is where the Environmentally Oriented store comes in and I am going to use The Design Galleria by Valentine in Sacramento, CA to show you what a "Best Store" can and should be like. Hopefully you will have a "Best Store" in your city or town; and I bet you do, if you will only look for it. But before I do this there is one critical thing you must do to be ready to shop in what I consider the "Best Store".

You must be prepared or, "Best Store" or not, you will not get the whole of what you want out of your shopping experience. I've talked about the kind of preparation you need to maximize each of your visits to any store; but with the environmentally oriented store you must really be prepared or you will miss the opportunity and often be more frustrated than ever with your furniture shopping. Be prepared: have your rooms plotted out, have a clear idea of what your budget is for each room. Be prepared to wait for the perfect items for your rooms. Be prepared to communicate to your designer/sales person exactly the feel or effect you want to achieve. Have a list of those items that you already own and want to continue using. Have a clear idea of how you want your rooms to function, and finally keep a good notebook on the items and ideas that have caught you eye during your planning stage. You're ready? OK let's meet the Design Galleria by Valentine in Sacramento, CA.

The Design Galleria by Valentine is housed in a beautiful three storied building with massive columns supporting a classic façade and painted a pale olive green with a very dark trim. It doesn't look like the typical furniture store, more like a southern plantation home or perhaps a Boston library. The owners, Bob Amaritto and Valarie Valentine, a husband and wife team, have a combined experience of furniture retailing of over 60 years. Bob was a senior executive with Macys's Department Stores and Valarie has been an interior designer in the Sacramento area for over 25 years. This long time experience in dealing with consumers has made them extremely sensitive to what consumers are looking for when shopping for furniture. And this experience plays a big role in how their store functions as a critical part of the consumer's goal to have a wonderful home. Staffed with 14 interior designers and 15 operation support people the store is open 7 days a week from 9 to 6, and by appointment anytime that works for both the staff and for the client. The interior display of the store is very full and very lush in its use of accessories and furniture items. Attractively lighted by both ceiling track lights and area lighting from the lamps on display, the whole effect is one of comfort and style. New items arrive weekly and are rotated on to the floor as display items are sold off. A critical difference between the Design Galleria by Valentine and the Item Store is that almost 90% of all merchandise orders received by Valentines are "special orders". Generally, the consumer will be waiting anywhere from one month to four months for their "special order" to be delivered and set-up in their home. This is one of the benchmarks of the environmentally oriented retail store. Most Item oriented retail stores deliver their customer orders within a week, to a month at most, to their client's homes. Of course you can walk into any of the environmental stores and buy a lamp or sofa or what-have-you and take an item home with you and conversely you can go into an Item Store and special order that sofa or bedroom and have to wait 6 weeks for delivery. This though is a very important difference and is at the base and foundation of how both kinds of stores operate and what that means to you.

Bob and Valerie's biggest day-to-day responsibility is to insure that their staff of 14 designers and 15 support people are working skillfully to insure that each client's individual goals and dreams for their home are being realized. This approach is not some casual effort but is the very foundation of the mission statement that Bob and Valerie insist their staff designers consider as the "bible" on how they conduct their business with a consumer. Every client is unique and every home is unique and thus every home plan is just that: a plan carefully prepared by clients with their designer to capture the whole effect that the client wants to achieve. It doesn't matter if the budget for the room is $2,000 or $20,000, the planning and attention to detail is the same. It doesn't matter if the plan is going to be implemented in one month or one year. The planning is the same and the planning is critical in bringing to fruition exactly what the client wants to accomplish. This is the big difference between the environmentally oriented store and the Item Store. I have said earlier in the book that it matters little what furniture items you select for your home if you do not plan well and pay attention to all of the other elements in your home: lighting, window coverings, accessories, paint, architectural details, room function, exterior views from your windows, exterior lighting, and your own personality and what you want to project with your home. All of these elements go into your plan; and remember, if you don't have a plan for a satisfying and enriching home, you automatically have a plan for just the opposite. The Design Galleria by Valentine's whole effort, from Mission Statement to implementation by their designers and staff, is to help you put your plan together. They then are able help you select the merchandise that best makes it happen. It takes time and a commitment from you and the designer to make it all happen. You can't do it in an afternoon. You can't do it if you don't share yourself and your dreams with the designer. The best results from the "Best Stores" are in the details and only you, with a skilled designer, can bring all of the details together in a wonderful whole for you. This is what a "Best Store" is all about. It is not about money. It is about value. The Design Galleria by Valentine is a "Value Added" store. The "Best Stores" in every city and town in the U.S. are "Value Added" stores. You save money when you get more value for every dollar you spend. Think about it. Remember the dollars you save will be your own.

I've spent a lot of time talking about the what I consider are the two types of furniture stores that you will encounter in your shopping simply because everything we have talked about in my book leads to just this point: the store. This is where everything you have learned will come into play and this is where everything the store is trying to accomplish comes into play. If you don't allow the store and its personnel to meet you half way you will not be able to benefit from their expertise that, coupled with yours, will spell savings and success. Let's take a look at some of the other "Best Stores" in the United States.

STORES YOU SHOULDN'T MISS!

I just shared with you **Furniture Today's Top 100 Stores in the United States** and it is always a fact that the marketplace votes on any player by the number of dollars that go through the door. Because the public votes this way, we can conclude that a lot of people are happy buying from these retail leaders. I now want to share with you a list of stores that are not volume leaders but are, in my opinion or in the opinion of people I respect, the best of the independents.

They may not be large stores, or major advertisers, or perfectly located, or have beautiful trucks—but do you know what they have? They have integrity. They have continuity. They have traditions. They have staff who have been with them for years. They have owners who insist on high standards of ethics and service. They care, and are relatively small enough to let you know they care. Their personnel have time to teach you about furniture. If you are within twenty miles of any of these stores, make it a point to go in and visit. I am sure that talking with the staff and looking over the store will assure you they do business the old-fashioned way: They work hard for you. By the way, I haven't ranked these stores in any way and I don't want to. The list is simply coming off the top of my head or the store has been recommended to me by my contacts in the industry. In short; the listing is in a way some of my favorite things. With apologies to Julie Andrews!

To begin this list of favorites I would say that any time I lived or shopped in an area that had an **Ethan-Allen Store, Thomasville Store, Drexel-Heritage Store**, and or a **La-Z-Boy Store**, or **BroyhillGallery**, I would make it a point to go in and see what they are up to. I always like to see what **Crate & Barrel** is showing. They are affordable and always have attractive clean-lined items to consider. **Cost Plus** is always worth a look. **Pier 1 Imports** is big with units all over the country, and while they are not your typical local store they certainly give you a price benchmark for attractive starter home furnishing items. I would also check out any of the major department store furniture selections. You would be making a mistake to not check them out. So who are the rest of my must see stores.

There is only one place to shop in **Alaska** and that is **Sadler's, William & Kays** and their **La-Z-Boy** outlet in **Anchorage**. All owned by Furniture Enterprises of Alaska. Nothing fancy, just good honest furniture housed in good honest stores. Hey, what are you going to do? Drive to Seattle to buy a sofa? Stay home and buy it at one of David Carvitt's stores.

If I were in **Seattle,** Washington, I would make it a point to shop **Masin's,** a family business carrying only the best of merchandise. Excellent staff, hands-on management, a total commitment to customer service—you will not do better. Now, does that mean you can go in there and find exactly what you want? Maybe not if you're looking for a specific product, but if you miss Masin's you may never know how well you can be treated. You should not miss **Ikea's Seattle** store. Big, different, affordable, very "shoppable".

If I'm still in **Washington State** and near the **Richmond** area, or in the **Spokane** area, I would go to the **Ennis Furniture Stores**. There's one in each of those cities, as well as in **Boise, Reno and Las Vegas**. This almost sounds like a chain in the making; but it is actually the Ennis family, doing their family thing, with the Ennis sons running the stores. They represent the best of what a local independent store can offer you—service, education, commitment, integrity, excellent pricing—and fun.

Never underestimate fun. If you are not having an enjoyable experience when shopping and buying furniture for your home, you have not been doing business with the right people.

In Oregon, in the **Portland** area, you must go to the **Paul Schatz Furniture Co**. They do it right and I don't think they have ever had an unhappy customer. You can't be in business for over fifty years unless you're doing right by your customers. Also in the Portland area is **Parker's Furniture Company**, another local merchant who does it right. Folks in Portland are lucky to have such solid local representation of the country's leading furniture manufacturers.

Moving down into California—in the **Sacramento** area are several excellent local independents. The previously mentioned **Design Galleria by Valentine** is sensational. Wonderfully displayed and loaded with top-drawer designers. This is a store that you should not miss. Another of my favorite stores is **Scofield's Furniture Company**. Frank and Virginia Scofield handle, for the most part, only the finest furniture, but they are such hands-on owners and managers that they can—and will—obtain any furniture a particular project warrants. Don't miss this store. Just getting to know the Scofields is reason enough for a visit, even if you don't buy any furniture.

Before I leave the capitol of the state, I wanted to mention **McCreery's Home Furnishings**, two large stores with a rather wide range of product and prices. The displays are good and the staff is energetic. They want to help. You would be missing a bet if you did not include McCreery's in your shopping. But before we leave Sacramento you have got to stop in **Naturwood Home Furnishings**. Two stores plus a wharehouse location and just loaded with good middle of the road merchandise. I don't mean that as a put-down. Naturwood is very much a super value store. If you don't stop by you are not shopping properly.

Our next stop in California is **Modesto**. Here you find **Slater's Home Furnishings**, a small store that features Drexel-Heritage furnishings, but a big store when it comes to design helpand design excitement. Tom Slater is an outstanding designer and product man. He knows his stuff and his staff know theirs. Don't miss Slater's.

Moving down the Great Central Valley of California, our next stop would be **Fresno**. I have three favorite stores in Fresno: **Berg Furniture Company**, which has been doing business there since 1910, and their next-door neighbor, **Slater's Furniture Co.**, which dates from 1912. By the way, Berg and Slater management are friends who share the same dedication to customer service. This two-stop shopping opportunity should not be missed. Another store you shouldn't miss is **Fashion Furniture**. A big solid middle of the road merchandiser. You can't shop Fresno well without stopping into Fashion Furniture.

Jumping over to the **San Francisco Bay** and **San Jose** area of California, we find about five million people—the fifth largest market area in the US—with surprisingly few good independent furniture dealers. **Flegel's** in Menlo Park is a particular favorite of mine for several reasons. The product selection is excellent—one of the larger Baker selections in the area and perhaps the largest dealer in the area of Stickley Furniture as well as Henredon and Guy Chaddock. Mark Flegel, the owner, is an absolute fanatic about customer care. He pampers his clients beyond belief. Good for the customers, but tough on his manufacturers, who have to adhere to a zero-tolerance level when it comes to quality control. Flegel's has two stores, one in **Menlo Park** and one in **San Rafael**. You must go into these stores and see one of the largest lineups of high-end product in the Bay area.

One of the more exciting players in the furniture game in the Bay area is **R.S. Basso.** This relatively new store, with outlets in **Palo Alto, Sebastopol, Healdsburg, St. Helena**, and **Danville**, is revolutionary in its approach to the furniture business. No discounts, no sales and no advertising. Mary Li and Ron Basso either flunked Business 101 or have a better idea—and they do have a better idea. It's called guts. They buy product they believe in. They display it well, and price it well the first time. Guess what has happened? The Basso stores are a major success. You don't need a house falling on you in order to see the lesson here—do it right the first time and people will recognize it. I hope more merchants will see what is happening at Basso and get the point. In the meantime, get over there and see what Ron and Mary are doing.

Don't dare leave the Bay area without shopping the **Suburban House Stores**, one each in **Cupertino and San Mateo and a new Wharehouse Showcase on Route 50.** The product line-up is upper end and wonderfully displayed. Backed up by a very solid design staff they are must-stops when you shop for furniture. Quality service and quality staff equal a quality experience. Don't miss it.

That last thought brought to mind an important point: No matter how big the store, or how big the selection of product, furniture-buying will ultimately boil down to a one-on-one experience between the client and the salesperson, or the client and the designer. One on one. The other eighty designers in the store, or the other eighty stores in the chain, will not affect your experience with that one person. It is that simple, and this is one reason why I love small independent furniture stores. After all, I am dealing with one man or one woman no matter where I am, so I like to seek out the smaller operation to begin with. The owners already know their physical operation is limited, so they don't rely on a sea of product to impress the client. They rely on themselves as individuals. Think about it. One good person and you—that is all you need in order to make your project a success.

Off to **Southern California** and its 29 million people. I don't know how many furniture stores, shops, design firms, outlets, etc., there are in this area, but it is a bunch! I can promise you that any furniture produced in this world can be found somewhere in Southern California. **Z Gallerie, Cost Plus, Pier One, Ikea,**

McMahan's, **The Leather Factory**, **Reeds Furniture**, and the list could go on an on. If you can't find what you want in Southern California you aren't looking.

When it comes to a large, well-run furniture operation, you can't beat a **Homestead House** store. They carry a wide selection of product from modest to expensive, have excellent customer service programs in place, and work hard for you. Now, this may not be an example of the small independent that I love so well and like to recommend, but Homestead House is run by a real gentleman. Dave Smith, despite the size of his business, is still very much an example of a merchant who really cares for his customer's satisfaction. Stop in and look around. You will be impressed.

This can't be the end of a section on LA, which has no end when it comes to consumer products. Books could be written on outlets in LA alone, but my purpose here is simply to tell you about my favorite stores. (Later I will tell you how I would be delighted to get you all the information you may want, on any store in any market.)

In **Hawaii** I have always like **C.S. Wo & Sons.** Shopping for furniture in Hawaii is always a challenge because of the very high freight costs that all of the merchants in the Islands have to contend with, and frankly your furniture costs are much highter in the Islands than they would be in any other state. This is the downside to living in Paradise. The upside is that a merchant like C.S. Wo & Sons works very hard to give you the local selection and local service that makes the higher prices still a value.

Off to Arizona. In **Phoenix** the store I like best—and it is a terrific store—is **Robb & Stucky.** With locations in Florida as well, R&S is run by one of the country's outstanding merchants, Clive Lubner. Clive has an eye for new product that is second to none, and his stores, while big, are wonderfully displayed and lavishly accessorized. His personal dedication and total commitment to excellence form the example that drives his staff to a level far beyond that of almost any other large operation. Get to a Robb & Stucky store and you will see what I mean. But don't let the glitter and glitz of Robb & Stucky blind you to a very solid, long time fixture in Phoenix—**M.D.Pruitt's.** Very big, solid, middle of the road merchandiser. The values are at M.D.Pruitt's and you should be to if you are looking to furnish your rental unit, or first home, or mountain cabin.

If we jump up to **Utah,** there is a very big operation that usually overwhelms me: **R. C. Willey.** The stores, about four of them, now part of the Berkshire Hathaway Corp, are huge—a sea of furniture to wade through. Again, why am I talking about one of the top twenty-five dollar-producers in this section about small independents? A good question. Like Dave Smith of LA's Homestead House, Bill Childs of R.C. Willey is a big operator with the heart and soul of a small independent. Bill grew up with the business and built the company with his brother and father. They did it all and never lost the personal touch. Their customers recognize this, and I believe it is a major reason why these stores have grown to dominate the whole state. In Utah it would be hard not to shop a Willey store. For all the size (and what that often entails elsewhere in the way of impersonal and distant atmosphere), R.C. Willey is still your local independent, there for you and ready to serve you.

In **Colorado,** we have the Denver area's major **Homestead House.** Yes, the LA area and Denver are where it all started for Homestead House—big, but not too big to make you feel at home. In LA or Denver, get to a Homestead House store. Of course you cannot miss the **American Furniture Warehouse**. The biggest furniture store system in Colorado and a very fine one at that for promotional to mid-priced furniture and bedding. Let's face it: if you need furniture or bedding and you don't want to mortage the house you have to go to the **American Furniture Warehouse**.

In **Denver** I also like **Davis and Shaw** because it is run by another of the industry's real gentlemen—Jon Jessop. Anything involving John is just plain good. This may not be the slickest store you have ever seen, but it will definitely be the most solid. Excellent merchandise, fine display, and customer service without equal.

In Texas, you must see **Louis Shanks.** With six stores spread around **Austin, Houston** and **San Antonio**, Shanks is a first-class operation, not big in the sense of a major chain but filled with a huge display of product from a few good manufacturers. They offer the best from no more than twenty manufacturers—Ralph Lauren to Lexington. Excellent display, very committed and competent staff. The ultimate in customer service. This isn't the only store in Texas, but it might be the only store you need. In **El Paso** is **Charlotte's Fine Furnishings**. This is the first store I visited in Texas back in 1963. Bob and Charlotte Willams had created a wonderful design gallery and today the family is still running a wonderful design gallery. Two stores now and very much an upper-end showcase. Don't miss it. In the **Rio Grande Valley** you have **Lack's** that (forgive me) lacks very little. Big and very broadly merchandised You really can't say you have shopped for furniture until you stop by their locations in the south of Texas. In **Houston** it is **Finger Furniture** and **Star Furniture** and they are all you need. Big, good, and capable of filling all your home furnishing needs. But don't neglect to stop by **Gallery Furniture** when you are in the Houston area. Gallery Furniture is unique when it comes to furniture operations. The owner, Jim McIngvale, is a "superstar" when it comes to promotions and promoting his business. **Edelstein's Better Furniture** in the **Brownsville** area has 14 stores and two designer showrooms that spans the furniture palette, from low end to Henredon and Century, and very much should be shopped. **Freed's Furniture Showcase** in **Dallas** has a good selection of some very exciting furniture out of China as well as mid-priced lines you will recognize. Always take a good look at the furniture that is coming out of the Far East. The values are there. **Dallas** also is the home of the contemporary specialist **Cantoni** which has stores in Southern California as well. You contemporary enthusiasts know how hard it is to find contemporary furniture in most market areas. Well Cantoni does it right. Make sure you stop in and look at what they have.

In **Oklahoma** it is definitely **Mathis Bros**. Big and broadly merchandised, you will find everything from starter items to Drexel-Heritage, Thomasville, Henredon, and even Ralph Laren. You simply cannot afford to miss Mathis Bros.

In **Kansas** the only place you must shop is **Benchmark Home Furnishings**. Very, very big. My heavens it is almost a half-million feet of merchandise! Benchmark is so big that consumers from all over the Mid-West are stopping in to see what's what. Now I constantly talk about the "wonders" of the small store where "everybody knows your name" and I personally like that kind of enviorment; but when it comes to shopping and getting to know what kind of merchandise is out there it is the Benchmark kind of store that can really give you an education. Remember though the bigger the store the more important it is for you to give the store salesman or woman a chance to really explain to you what a Benchmark kind of store can do for you and your budget.

The **Nebraska Furniture Mart** in **Omaha, Nebraska** has become an "institution" and truly an inspiration for all furniture merchants in the U.S. You should stop by even if you do not need any homefurnishing items. It has been so well run for so many years that consumers in the Mid-West simply make it a must shop experience. Warren Buffet, one of our country's best "merchants" liked it so much that he ended up buying the whole store! You can't do that anymore but you would be making a mistake if you didn't stop by to see what they have for your family room.

In **Wisconsin** there is the vernerable **Porter Furniture**. My heavens it has been in business since 1857 and carries the very best of American furniture: Stickley, Henredon, Baker, Kindle, Karges, and Drexel Heritage. They can do it all for you and if you miss it, not only will you miss what has become an institution, but you will miss a well run family business. Trust me: shop Porter's.

In **Michigan** I like **Gorman's Home Furnishings**. They have run good stores for many years now. Mid-priced to upper-end product from Drexel Heritage, Century, and Bernhardt. Well worth a look.

I have a favorite store in **Chicago: Plunketts Furniture Co.** They also have a wonderful store in **St. Louis**, but I think of Chicago when I think of Plunketts. They now have three or four stores in the Chicago area. The large Plunketts family is involved in all of them, and in all phases of the business. Good display, outstanding sales and design staff, a wide range of mid- to upper-end furniture. Plunketts is a total package for a complete and exciting furniture-shopping experience. Don't miss it. And you shouldn't miss **Harlem Furniture** with fourteen stores in **Metro Chicago**. A large mid-priced chain that is perfect for the newly weds starting their first homes as well as anyone who is simply looking for good values and sensible furniture.

In **Ohio** and **Indiana** it is **Kittle's** and rightly so. From promotional furniture to high-end furniture, Kittle's has it all. A well run chain that is nicely displayed and well staffed. Don't need to drive to Chicago when you have a Kittle's store in your neighborhood.

In the **Central Pennsylvania** area there is a family enterprise called **Lush Brothers**. I'm prejudiced because I love this family but, after that admission, I must say they run a great group of stores—about four of them, all well worth seeking out. Excellent merchandise, great staff, and a real home-town approach to customer care. Make sure you stop in. Of course there is more to Pennsylvania than just my buds at Lush Brothers. **Oskar Huber Furniture,** with stores in **Valley Forge** and **Southhampton** and even spills over into **New Jersey** with a store in **Ship Bottom** and **Cherry Hill**. They have **La-Z-Boy Galleries** in all of their stores and that is reason enough to shop them. **Levin Furniture** in the **Pittsburgh** area is big, affordable, and well done. In **Philadelphia** you should stop by **Diamond Furniture**. Not a big chain and not a fancy chain, but an honest chain of six stores. Good place to look when you don't want to spend a lot of money but you do want furniture that can stand up to a growing family.

In **Boston**, it's **Jordans**. They have been excellent for years and continue to be so. **Boston Interiors** with five stores is not big but a good combination of value and style. Well worth a look. **Raymour & Flanigan** cover the **Northeast** like a blanket and where they aren't **Huffman Koos** or **Good's** is. Mid-priced to high-end, these chains bring selection and values to the local markets.

In **New York City,** like LA, you can find any furniture produced on this planet. In major metro areas there is no end to the number of outlets for you to shop. There are two, though, that I make a point to visit because they are always doing something extra in a grand way. Both **Bloomingdale's** and **ABC Carpets** are exciting, solid, cutting-edge operations. The wonderful aspect of these stores is that they are not only definitive furniture shops but also fun shops. Fun, excitement, the joy of discovery, all blended with quality and qualified help—what more could you want? Well, in New York no matter what you want it is there.

Leaving New York, let's pop on down to **Atlanta,** Georgia. Atlanta is getting to be like NYC. They have it all when in comes to furniture. Atlanta is also within striking distance to the North Carolina wholesale/retail outlets and this presents a challenge to not only the Atlanta furniture stores but also to the consumers in the Atlanta market area. If having a wonderfully furnished home was simply a matter of buying furniture at the lowest possible price then there probably wouldn't be any furniture stores in Atlanta, but as you know this isn't the case. Discounts do not create beautiful homes. My favorite store over the years in Atlanta has been **Flack's Interiors**. Run by Hilda Flack, and I mean run by Hilda Flack, this is a smaller operation in physical terms, but run by one of the industry's biggest personalities. I understand Hilda is opening a new operation in the city that will be a Drexel-Heritage Showcase Store scheduled to open in the late Spring of 2004. You must stop by and see what she is up to. Hilda Flack is show business; but, more than that, she is brilliant show business, and she demands the same performance from her staff. If I were within five hundred miles of a Hilda Flack store, I would consider it my hometown store.

I mentioned Robb & Stucky in Arizona, but they started their wonderful traditions in Florida and then expanded to Arizona. In **South Florida, Robb & Stucky** is, for me, the place to shop. Winter visitors from the northeast, jaded from living in the midst of so many choices, find a Robb & Stucky store takes the furniture shopping experience to a whole new level. Robb & Stucky does it right. A close furniture associate of mine tells me that **El Dorado Furniture** in **South Florida** is as exciting a furniture store as you will see any place in the U.S. With seven stores and unlimited imagination coupled with a real sense of theater, the Capo family have created furniture excitement. I will be going there soon to see what all the buzz is about. I think you better stop by soon yourself. Actually Florida seems to be generating more excitement when it comes to furniture than is the case in most other states. Along with Robb & Stucky, and El Dorado Furniture you also have to always shop **Baer's**, with 14 stores, and **Carls** with 16 stores. With all this going on the Florida consumer has the best of all possible worlds when it comes to shopping for furniture.

This has been a brief list of my favorite stores—stores with personality, run by strong leaders who are real merchants. Even if the stores are big, like Homestead House or R.C. Willey, they reflect that leadership. Major chains (run by countless committees, by layer upon layer of management that insulate and isolate the leader from the led) often have no clearcut mandate beyond profit. Now profit is not bad but, when it becomes the store's middle name, it dilutes those characteristics that made the business big. It is ironic that the lessons and paths that led to success are forgotten or ignored.

There are wonderful stores in every part of the country—stores unfamiliar to you, perhaps, but that are right in your own home town. Take this little test: Quickly, name five furniture stores in your city, and then name five furniture manufacturers. I'll bet eighty per cent of you flunked the test. So I am going to make an offer: If you request information about stores or furniture—or have any question concerning the furniture experience—I will be glad to help you make good choices. Contact me at www.newfurnitureideas.com, or mail a letter to my publisher (whose address is toward the front of this book), who will forward it to me.

Now after all of the above and all of the preceeding you haven't done the unthinkable, have you? **Please don't do this? You did?** What I am talking about is a small ad that ran in U.S.A. Today on August 22, 2003. This is what the ad had to say: "Furniture Shopping! Buy direct from N.C. Inside set-up Nationwide. Over 400 mfg. Savings up to 50%" and then they gave a 1-800 number. I am not going to give you the phone number because this is not the way to buy furniture or to save money.

Why? Well how much do you know about furniture? You just bought this book (and a good one it is; but!) and I am wondering how much you know about furniture and what makes any piece of furniture a "Good Buy"? To begin with, in today's world you can find all the furniture you want at discounts up to 50% off in your hometown. Every furniture store today is a "discounter"! Yep! Everyone of them. There was a time, say 25 years ago when your local stores were not as heavily discounted as the stores in say North Carolina, but that is no longer the case.

You will find ads like the one above in most magazines devoted to the home (Shelter Magazines), many newspapers, and occasionally even in airline magazines. This kind of mind-set, simply looking for a discount, is the surest way to spend more money than you need to and often to flat-out waste your money. Until you know what makes one item better than another how can you possibly know if a discount on any item is a good way for you to go?

I hope by the time you have read this book you will have a better perspective on buying any furniture item and will not be a dewy-eyed consumer ready to fall for any advertising gimmick that you come across. Trust me: a 50% off ad for furniture in some obscure store in some distant state is not going to change your life or your pocket book for the better. Who are these guys?

THE NORTH CAROLINA DISCOUNTER

Should you use the North Carolina trans-shipper, the 800 number, the Discounters? All these terms or codes refer to the same thing—the Big Discount Store in North Carolina.

Is it real or is it a myth? It is a myth and it is real. How can that be? The myth is that the deals are so good you just have to use them. This could be true if having a beautiful home required nothing more of you than buying expensive furniture at a big discount, but I have seen many unattractive rooms furnished by people who bought discounts only and then wondered why their home didn't sparkle.

Purchasing the furniture is only one step in the quest for that perfect look and, while it is the most expensive step, it too often is the step to which the least thought is given.

You cannot pick up a shelter magazine (a magazine devoted to the home) without seeing classified advertisements offering big discounts from hundreds of furniture manufacturers. You even see these ads in many newspapers. There is no doubt that we all like a good deal, and we all need to buy as sharply as we can, but my whole purpose in writing this small book is to convince you to stop shopping for discounts and start shopping for values. If you have decided to do business with an out-of-state discounter, you will find that your financial arrangement with them is only as stable as their business. Don't ever assume that just because someone runs an ad in a slick magazine or newspaper that they are financially sound. It would be very wise of you ascertain the stability of a store before you do business with it. Call the state's BBB, or local agencies that could help you decide how safe it is to deal with a company unknown to you.

The supposed benefits of doing business with a North Carolina discounter are that you may receive a better price and you do not pay a sales tax. The risks are that the furniture may not be quite what you expected; the store may not be financially sound and you could lose your deposit; your local retailer may not honor any guarantees on the furniture, and you will have to deal with the trucking company that delivers the item. Now after saying all that there are three major stores in the High Point, Hickory, and Charlotte areas that deserve to be shopped. Retailers across the nation often consider them "The Enemy" and they are often called by the trade "Discounters!", but they are a long way from a dirty-window discounter where you have to watch your wallet and your step. **Furnitureland South, Boyles Furniture**, and **Rose Furniture** are the three stores in North Carolina that I think are the best, most reliable, most honest, and biggest displayers of furniture product in the state. You should shop all three. Not because of the discounts—you could probably get the same discounts at your local store—but because they all have huge assortments of furniture items on display and are often in a better position than out-of-state stores to get extra cost savings off of production furniture from, for them, the local manufacturers. In fairness to the North Carolina stores, there is often a sales tax advantage in doing business with them; but this isn't the fault of the Carolina stores. The tax problem is one for your local politician to contend with, not you or the stores. At the moment it works to your advantage, but for heavens sake add up all the pluses and minuses before you make a decision.

Do you know what "Churrigueresque Furniture" is? Contact me at www.newfurnitureideas.com and I'll tell you. Hey, this is a test to see if you are reading my book!

Often the difference between a San Francisco price for an item that will be delivered to your home, as opposed to an item that you could buy from a North Carolina dealer at a fancy "discount", and then have to pay the shipping costs from there, may not be all that different. Remember, the key is always to be comparing apples to apples and not apples to oranges. Do your homework and compare all the costs before you decide. So should you fly off to High Point to save a bundle? Well, the bundle will not be that big in my estimation; but if you throw in the need for some Carolina Bar-B-Q the trip will be well worth the time. Keep in mind that now every furniture store in the United States is a "discounter". Everyone of them. The question today isn't "Who are the discounters?" or "Where are the discounters?"; the question is "What is the discount?" What a sorry state of affairs! Sorry in that the whole adventure of making your home wonderful is reduced to a "discount"! When everybody discounts nobody discounts! A little Zen for you there. If anyone gets to that sentence and wants me to explain it, visit my website at www.newfurnitureideas.com and drop me a line.

To be a good shopper, to save significant money on your furniture purchases, to recognize how retail furniture stores function, to select the best designer for you—all require you to do your homework and not to think that buying furniture is simply looking for the biggest discount. Your first homework assignment was to read this book. Your next assignment is to enjoy the fascinating world of furniture. Hey! You're going to love it now that you have the tools to play the game.

11

ADVERTISING

Reading Between the Lines Helps You Become a Smarter Shopper!

It is Saturday morning in Anytown, U.S.A. Your wife or significant other is complaining about the sofa in the den—the one your mother gave you ten years ago. What do you do? Well, fortunately, you just read my book. Now you know what to do, so let's get specific:

It is Saturday morning in Folsom, California. I pick up the morning paper and look for the furniture advertisements. If I tell you what my local furniture stores are saying to me, I'll bet your local stores are saying the same things to you. Let's see if we have more insight now than we had when we started the book.

I wrote those two paragraphs for the first edition of the book and here we are about five years later and almost nothing has changed when it comes to advertising furniture in the newspapers or magazines except the prices and the dates. You may still have the sofa your mother gave you and you are in even more trouble now after waiting fives years to solve the problem. We had better start shopping and like most consumers the first thing we do is to look at the local ads. What are they saying?

Incidentally, I am reading my local newspaper, "The Sacramento Bee". Let's see: here is the first ad on page 2: "Endless Summer" is the headline and then we see "Patio Furniture Clearance: Buy Now and Choose: Extra 10% Off or 1 Year Free Financing* No Down, No Payments, No Interest. Up to 50% off: Hurry! Many Quantities are Limited. 5pc Dining Sets: 48" round umbrella table w/4 dining chairs". The ad then goes on and lists 9 pictures of 5 piece patio dining sets from different manufacturers showing discounts of 25%, 30% or 50%. This was an ad from "California Backyard" which has four locations and is my favorite outdoor patio items store in the region. But what have we been told by this ad? Nothing except you had better hurry to buy and the discounts are up to 50% off. We learned nothing about patio furniture except that this dealer is running a sale. What would have been nice to learn is whether or not the items shown were plastic, or wood, or metal. Did the umbrella table have a plastic top or tempered glass? Are the finishes on the items warranted for any length of time? In short we learned little of value beyond the price that is advertised, and while this is important, it is more important for you to know a great deal more than the price of an item if you are going to be a Smart Shopper. Let's go on.

"Naturwood Furniture Company", a big local retailer (a very good local retailer as a matter of fact), has a full-page ad with a big happy face telling us that there is "Zero Interest till 2005" or 10% off. This kind of ad is repeated across the county with minor variations, but what I want to point out to you is the typical small print at the bottom of the page that you should be familiar with when considering "No Interest" kinds of sales. Keep in mind that this is not unique to Naturwood nor is it illegal or even shady. These are the facts and these facts will be true across the country with local variations as to the actual percentage rates and minimum rules. Here is the fine-print: "No interest until 2005 is based on approved credit, a minimum $500 purchase, 30% down payment and monthly payments. If balance and/or monthly payment are not paid in full by end of term, interest is retroactive to date of receipt at 21.9% APR. Offer not available in conjunction with any other sale prices or any factory authorized promotions. **10% off regular price on in-stock merchandise, except already reduced items and TempurPedic products. Offer ends 9/14/03". Now this is full disclosure and this is exactly what you need to know but make sure you read every thing in an ad and on a contract or you could end-up very surprised and possibly hurting. Incidentally, this is not a swipe at Naturwood Furniture Company. Any advertiser using this kind of promotion must disclose all of the particular details as per state regulations.

NOT A DIME. YOU DON'T PAY UNTIL '06, NO MONEY DOWN, NO MONTHLY PAYMENT, NO INTEREST CHARGES.

We next come to an ad on page 9 from "Scandinavian Designs" that is showing a 6 Seat Microfiber Sectional for $1444. The ad tells us that this sectional is shown in a blue or sand microfiber that "combines noticeable softness with a refined silk-matte texture. It then tells us "that any soiling remains on the surface to be easily removed." Wow? Wouldn't it be nice to know what kind of soiling they are talking about? Wine? Motor-oil? Jelly? Perhaps peanut butter? Do they tell us what "microfiber" is? No. The ad goes on to mention that the Bedford Leather Recliner is $695 while the Olympus Leather Recliner is $199 and the Dover Leather Recliner is $399. Now each of these recliners is shown with an ottoman in the picture. Does the advertised price include the pictured ottoman? We just don't know. And in the very small print under each picture we read that each "Leather" Recliner has a "matching vinyl back"! Give me a break! A "leather" chair does not have a vinyl back. A combination leather and vinyl chair can have a vinyl back but not a "leather" chair. Now Scandinavian Design is a respected store. They do not have to stoop to this kind of "shady" advertising. It is not a big thing but it reminds us that it is WE that need to be prepared to be smart furniture shoppers because the stores and the industry is doing its best to not fully inform us as to what they are up to.

On we go to page 11 and we find an ad from "The Leather Factory". The head-line reads "Factory Direct Leather Sale!" Right in the middle of the ad we read that "50% off the chair or recliner and 1 year free financing". We are told that this is "custom-made to fit your home and family". "We make it, we sell it, we ship it....You Save". We learn that this is 100% Top Grain Leather in your choice of 100 colors. What we don't learn is what the prices are! Fascinating! They go on to tell us that their leather items are 100% American made furniture direct from the manufacture for less. Now this could be good news or non-news. The fact that their items are American made tells us nothing about the quality; and without any prices mentioned we can not compare their prices with other stores' prices.

The Leather Factory has about 17 stores in the West. You will not run into them in say Boston, but you will run into a similar type of leather supplier trumpeting the fact that they have nothing but American made product. Is this fact of "American Made" a plus for you or not? Well the political answer is yes. It is good for Americans to buy American products because when we buy "American" it sup-ports our own industries and our own stores. This very fact helps each of us in "Everytown" U.S.A. Unfortunately, from a purely consumer standpoint, you can save money buying leather product that is now flooding into our local stores from China, Europe, Mexico, and South American. Bottom-line—you will save money buying this kind of product, and it can be a very good product, but is it the right thing to do? Only you can answer that question. My job is to make you aware of the increasing number of choices that you have as con-sumers. The world is changing. Globalization is a buzzword that has infi-nite connotations from good to bad. Time will tell if "The World As A Village" is a good idea or a nightmare. Right now you can buy furniture with more style and with excellent quality features at better prices than ever before. But it may not be American!

The next ad we come to is on pages 12 and 13. By George, it is a "double truck" (two page ad), to lay an advertising term on you. The ad is from "Room Source" and they tell us they are "The Central Valley's Largest Volume Furniture Store". You have the same type of big box, big volume store in your area. The name of the store changes from location to location across the county but the concept is the same: big lower-end selection with heavy orientation in their presentations to financial considerations rather than furniture details. This is not bad, it simply is the way they do business.

MARCH OAK MADNESS

YOU DON'T NEED A CORNER OFFICE TO HAVE A GREAT VIEW

Let's take a look at some of the questions that arise when you read their ad. There is a 100% Solid Pine Loft Bed shown for $697.88 or $22 a month on approved credit. Now does 100% Solid Pine mean anything important to you? Not really. What type of pine are they talking about? Sugar Pine? Baltic Pine? Perhaps one of the other 100 or so pines in the forest. How was the pine handled? Was it kiln-dried to 5%? In short: 100% of any wood does not tell us anything that is really important for us to make a quality decision on. Another pictured item tells us that we could have a "Queen-Size, Antiqued, Washed Pine Slat Bed" for $387.88 or $15 a month on approved credit. Frankly, I am not sure what a Washed Pine Slat Bed means. Does it mean that the slats that the mattress rests on are pine and the rest of the bed is made out of different wood? It might. What does "Washed Pine" mean? I expect this term relates to the finish but the picture doesn't suggest this. Keep in mind that sometimes the picture used in an ad doesn't show the item or items that are offered at the sale price. They should, and when they are not the picture should indicate this, but sometimes mistakes are made.

The final item in their ad that I want to bring to your attention is a Leather-Match sofa that is offered at $597.88 or $19 a month on approved credit. The sofa is described as a "100% Top Grain Leather on all Seating Areas". This means that leather is used on just the top of the cushion and the facing outsides of the pillows. The rest of the sofa is upholstered in something else which is usually a matching vinyl. Is this bad? No, but don't get confused when you compare this type of leather sofa with a leather sofa that is all leather clad. Be on the alert any time you see terms like: Leather-Match, Leather-Mate, Leather-Pal, Leather-Buddy or any other term that could indicate that the item is not upholstered fully in leather. The fact that an item is not fully upholstered in leather is not "Bad" it simply means that a major cost saving method was used by the manufacturer to keep the price of the item down. This could be a real plus for you. It also could be a confusing factor for you if you don't keep all your information ducks and geese in order when you are shopping. Read all ads carefully and then be prepared to ask good questions of the salesperson who is helping you.

The next ad we come to on page 15 is from Beck's Furniture Company— a large, local merchant that concentrates on middle to lower-end furniture. His ad brings to our attention several common problems that occur often in furniture ads across the country. We see that Beck's is advertising a "Cherry Traditions Bedroom", a three-piece set, for $398. To begin with the "three piece set" is actually the three components of the bed! The headboard, footboard, and metal rails! Come on now. These three components are not three different items they collectively make up the bed that is pictured so it isn't a three-piece set, it simply is the bed. Next we read that the bedroom pictured is the "Cherry Traditions Bedroom". Does that mean the bedroom is constructed out of cherry wood or veneers? Not necessarily so, to paraphrase George Gershwin. It could mean the bedroom has a cherry finish on any kind of wood; or it could mean that the group name is simply that—a name only. Going on we see leather sofas featured at $698 to $998 and sofas in fabric from $398 to $598. We learn that some of the fabrics for sale are "DuraPella" which is a trademarked name for probably a microfiber. We don't know that as a fact but I suspect it is. We see recliners for $398 again featured in the "DuraPella" super tough fabric. Again we have on the one hand seemingly a great deal of information but in reality what we have are a great deal of questions. Now, in all fairness, any ad is calculated to do just that. The advertiser wants you to be so interested in what he has to say that you simply must go into the store to get the full answers. Hey, this is what business is all about. And this is why you must be a very well prepared shopper in order to make really good decisions.

On page 18 we run into a big ad from American Furniture, a retailer that has three stores in the Sacramento area, and their ad highlights a common ploy by furniture merchants, in particular, to get you to come into their store. In huge red print we see "Final Days, 3 million dollars in furniture inventory must go this weekend!" We also see that "All furniture ordered sold off immediately". Not sure what that sentence really means but I gather you better watch out or you could be run over by deliverymen carrying a sofa out the door. Now for the clincher of a statement we see repeated ten or more times that this is a "Public Authorized Furniture Sell Off". What does that mean? Does it mean the store is going out of business? No. Does it mean that the store is changing hands and a new owner is taking over? No. Does it mean anything? Not really. What the store is trying to do is to make you think that something very special is going on and that may be true or it may not be true. It could be that the prices shown are simply the routine prices for that store. I don't care where you live in the U.S.A., you routinely see ads like this one. Sometimes they do mean the store is going out of business and a better deal than normal may be in order, but most often they are simply advertising hype and offer you little more than you normally get from the merchant. Remember, the more shrill the ad the more careful you want to be when considering whether or not you want to run over to the store. You could be wasting your time.

STORE-WIDE SAVINGS UP TO 1/2 OFF

The next ad is on page 20 and it is a full-page ad by the local La-Z-Boy Furniture Galleries. La-Z-Boy is advertising its 20th Anniversary with special prices on recliners from $298.88 to $998.88 and slipcover sofas at $999.98. They make the point that you should come on in and talk with their experienced sales staff. The nice thing about La-Z-Boy nationwide is that their sales staff is knowledgeable. La-Z-Boy management works hard to see that this is true. The product is honest. The prices are reasonable, and the commitment to quality service is there. Bottom-line: you rarely will make a mistake doing business with La-Z-Boy.

The final ad that I am going to mention in this newspaper review is from one of the local Ethan Allen Gallery Stores. It is a small ad on page 21 and it illustrates the remaining common approach used by the higher-end furniture stores across the country. The ad simply says "Extended Labor Day Sale" with it ending on Sunday September 7th. There are a few details as to what is and isn't on sale, and a comment that the savings range from 10% to 50% on clearance merchandise throughout the store. No prices are mentioned in the ad. I love the Ethan Allen Stores. They consistently do a good job of training their people and they consistently bring quality furniture at good prices to their floors. You will not go wrong doing business with Ethan Allen either.

So where does all this leave us? I did spend a lot of time talking about furniture advertising for several reasons. The most important reason why an understanding of furniture advertising is so important is that the furniture ad in the newspaper is usually the first place we look when we wake up and realize we need some new furniture. But something new in our lifestyles has occurred that I think is shifting our perspectives when it comes to a lot of merchandise not just furniture. This new awareness is coloring how we look at furniture ads and how we look at furniture itself when we walk into our local retailers. The new factor in our lifestyles? Well I believe it is the rise of the Big Box Super Stores like Wal-Mart, Costco, Sam's Club, Price Club, etc. You know the kind of stores I am referring to. Most of us have one in our neighborhood and for the first time since the advent of a Sears Roebuck type of store this new Super Store is making us aware of a broader spectrum of merchandise at very good prices. It is a fact that no matter what our economic circumstances we all are shopping these Super Stores. All of a sudden the consumer who arrives at the Super Store in his or her BMW to pick-up paper products walks by several leather sofas that are on sale for $699. All leather and on sale for $699! Amazing. We then stroll past a good looking dining room table and 4 chairs that is on sale for $999! Amazing! We go on and buy a year's supply of Kleenex and off we go, but along with the Kleenex we are carrying an impression that a leather sofa costs around $699 and we could have a dining table and chairs for around $999!

It is amazing but it also is only part of the story. Not too long ago we were much more of a "provincial" sort of shopper. We generally shopped in those stores that our "crowd" shopped in. You were either the BMW Crowd, or the Buick Crowd, or VW Crowd, and because of this "crowd" approach we generally were unaware of a great deal of differently priced merchandise. But with the rise of the Super Store many of us are, at the very least, becoming aware of a great deal of new merchandise that is not only modestly priced but wonderfully attractive and of a very decent quality. Now does this mean that all of a sudden we don't shop in the stores that used to attract us. Of course not. We still shop in the same stores we used to; but our perspective is much more sophisticated. We are not slaves to a "Crowd" look anymore. Ralph Lauren, Martha Stewart, Wal-Mart, Costco, all have contributed to expanding our appreciation levels for wonderful products that are often modestly priced. Into this heady mix of growing sophistication came an emerging global sup-

HUGE SAVINGS WHEN YOU BUY BY THE ROOM

ply chain for products at prices greatly reduced from their traditional levels. The consequences of this new revolution at retail are still not fully understood, and all of the consequences will not be pleasant; but at the moment it is a plus for all of us consumers. My book is concerned with the whole story and unless you carefully read this book you are going to be more confused than ever when it comes to shopping for furniture.

Let me say it again: never have we as consumers had so many choices when it comes to furniture and never have we had such a wide price variance without the usual sacrifice in quality as we have today. In many respects it is the "Best of Times"; but the flip-side of the "Best of Times" is the worst of times for many local manufacturing companies. Hopefully a balance can be found to allow for all the elements of our supply chain to be healthy and prosperous. But for you and me! Be prepared and it will be the "Best of Times" for you and your home.

GOOD LUCK:
50% OFF!

12

LEARNING MORE ABOUT IT ALL!
You Already Know How to Shop!

The most important thing to remember is this: You are a better furniture shopper than you think you are. Everything you know about the fundamentals of quality and value (in clothes, cars, jewelry, etc.) applies to furniture selection. If you are new to furniture shopping, all you need, in order to be an expert, is to know the furniture vocabulary, the quality points to look for, and the way the furniture world works. I hope this small book has helped equip you with that knowledge and, more importantly, I hope I've given you a hint of the fascination of furniture.

Some wag in the industry years ago said, "Only the rich can afford to buy cheap furniture." I agree with the sentiment. I hope you now understand what I mean when I say that the discovery of wonderful furniture items, new, old, modest, or expensive, is a journey of discovery—of yourself and of those objects that reflect your personality. Don't be trapped by the expectations of others or the latest buzz words and hip solutions. We are talking about your home and, with permission, "A home is a terrible thing to waste."

What follows is not a bibliography. It is a list of magazines and books that I believe will make your shopping more fun and increase your appreciation of furniture and the home. These are titles you can find in any city in the United States, if not the world. I consider these the best of all publications devoted to the home.

Before I begin, I must admit that I am a little worried about listing magazines and books as a resource guide. Why? Because, as you browse through shelter magazines, the overwhelming impression you may get is that wonderful rooms cost a lot of money. Well they can, but they don't have to. I hope you don't fall into this common trap: first, we look; second, we fall in love; third, we check the price; fourth, we fall out of love, and never again believe our homes can be just as exciting as any home pictured in the best magazines. Remember this: Spend your imagination lavishly, but spend your money wisely. Excitement, warmth, comfort—all can be had without destroying your budget.

I can remember reclining on a large, sloping, river rock, worn smooth by eons of weather and water. I was looking out over a river as it roared down from the western Carolina mountains on a warm fall day. I had just had a good lunch and I lay there thinking: "How much more comfortable could I ever be?" After two weeks at the High Point International Furniture Market, selling sofas that would retail for $2,500 or more, I realized that not one of them "sat better" than that river rock— no springs, no padding, no frame, no fabric, yet it fit me like a glove. I hadn't spent one dime for the comfort of that moment. Don't miss the point I've emphasized throughout this whole book: Money isn't the answer to wonderful rooms or homes. With this in mind, let's take a look at the lists.

MAGAZINES

Art & Antiques: One of my favorite magazines. You don't have to be a lover of antiques. This magazine is full of information about many objects you will find in your travels.

Architectural Digest: One of the best of all the magazines devoted to fine homes and interiors. Even though the homes featured are beyond most of us, the techniques and ideas are not.

Better Homes & Gardens: They do so many special editions on so many elements of the home that they are a must to review. I have yet to see an issue that wasn't beautifully done.

Country Home: I like it for the warmth and coziness demonstrated by their features. You don't have to be a country fan to get real solid information and ideas from their spreads.

Colonial Homes: Like Country Home, it is an inviting and provocative look at a more simple lifestyle that still appeals to many of us today.

Country Accents: I just can't get enough of this genre. Again, I get ideas that stretch me.

Elle/Decor: Both the British and French publications are fascinating but I don't read French so I am always limited to the pictures in that edition. However, in either language, the message of style comes across.

House Beautiful: Filled with ideas and suggestions that make you a more knowledgeable, well-informed shopper.

Home Beautiful, Home Remodeling and **Decorating:** Ideas, ideas, ideas. The more you look through the shelter magazines, the more options you begin to have. They stretch your imagination.

House & Garden: Two of my favorite topics in one magazine. Always well done. You should read it every month.

Homes & Garden: (British) I love Great Britain and I am always ready to read anything about their gardens. They do them well.

Inspirations For Your Home: I read this magazine for the first time recently and enjoyed it very much. Good ideas throughout.

Interior Design: Very much for the more serious home enthusiast. Thrust is toward the professional, but any student of the home should read this magazine often.

Mary Englebreit's Home Companion: Is a charming look at the home. Beautifully done and filled with wonderful extras that can help make rooms come alive.

Metropolitan Home: I always enjoy MH even though I am a traditionalist. I never fail to get a good idea from each issue.

Old House Interiors: As you can see, I never get enough of old houses. A solid piece. I always check their ads and classifieds.

Southern Accents: You don't have to live in the South to enjoy this magazine. Let's face it, there is a style in the South that I find quite seductive. Southerners enjoy their homes.

Southern Living: As with SA, I simply like to see what is happening in this most comfortable of regions.

Sunset: The magazine for Westerners. It doesn't contain enough about furniture, but I always check the gardening advice.

Traditional Style: This is one of Better Homes and Gardens' publications and it is excellent. BH&G does a beautiful job with special-interest pieces. Always take a look at them.

The New Decorating Book: Another Better Homes & Gardens publication. This one is excellent and will really help you get oriented before starting your home project.

Victorian: Not my cup of tea when it comes to design, but I always like to pick up this magazine and see what they have to say.

Veranda: New for me, but very slick. I expect to see more of this magazine.

Do I buy all of these magazines every month? No, but I buy most of them, and I rarely let too many months go by without catching up on the ones I missed. I just can't encourage you enough—read these magazines when you are dreaming or shopping for your home. They will stretch your imagination and give you solid advice on having fun while solving problems.

BOOKS

The following is a list of some of the furniture-related books I keep on my shelves at home. All of them are wonderful aids when you are furniture-shopping or design-planning and want facts right at your fingertips.

Beginnings of Interior Environment by Phyllis S. Allen, Brigham Young University Press, Provo, Utah, 1977

Country Living/Country Decorating by Bo Niles, Hearst Books, New York, 1988

Designing Furniture by Seth Stem, The Taunton Press, Newtown, Conn., 1989

Feng Shui by Angel Thompson, St Martin's Press, New York, 1996

Interior Design and Decoration by Sherrill Whiton, J.B. Lippincott Co., New York, 1974

Interior Design by John F. Pile, Harry N. Abrams, Inc., New York, 1988

Modern Wood Finishing Techniques by Noel Johnson Leach, Linden Publishing, 1997

The Bed by Alecia Beldegreen, Stewart, Tabori, & Chang, New York, 1991

The Complete Manual of Wood Veneering by William A. Lincoln, Linden Publishing, 1984

The Decoration of Houses by Alexandra Stoddard, William Morrow & Co., New York, 1997

The New Fine Points of Furniture by Albert Sack, Crown Publishers, New York, 1993

The National Trust Manual of Housekeeping by H. Sandwith & S. Stainton, Penguin, 1991

The Sensual Home by Ilse Crawford, Rizzoli International, New York, 1997

Understanding Wood Finishing by Bob Flexner, Rodale Press, Emmaus, PA., 1994

World Woods in Color by William Lincoln, Linden Publishing, Fresno, CA, 1990

TO THE READER

Thank you so much for your interest in this book. I hope you will find it to be a truly helpful tool as you shop for furniture. But the help doesn't stop with the book. I am dedicated to being an on-going resource for information on home furnishings and related matters. I do not sell any type of home furnishing product because I intend to remain an independent and unbiased source of information to the consumer.

You can talk to me about any of your questions or concerns by visiting my website - www.newfurnitureideas.com - where there is complete contact information. I will be delighted to help you in any way I can. YOU NOW HAVE A PARTNER IN THE FURNITURE BUSINESS!

Thank you and good shopping!
Leonard B. Lewin

P.S. If you're a designer, teacher, furniture store, or other interested party, the publisher of the book, Linden Publishing, will be happy to discuss giving you a quantity discount. They can be reached at 1-800-345-4447.

INDEX

A

Acacia, 30, 34
Acrylic, 76
Action, 36, 86-87, 93-94
Adams, 3, 8
American Drew, 101
Aniline. *See* Dye
Antiques, 7-8, 45-46, 92, 131
Armoire, xi, 46, 49, 50, 53, 96
Art Nouveau, 6, 8
Arts and Crafts, 6, 8, 10, 104
Ash, 30, 38

B

Back panel, 21
Back pillows, 63, 66, 72
Baker furniture, 101
Barcalounger, 94
Bassett, 78, 101-102, 104, 106
Bed, 28, 49-50, 53, 96, 126, 133. *See also* Mattress
Beeswax, 34
BenchCraft, 90, 94
Berkline, 94
Bernhardt, 102, 118
Books, 96, 116, 130, 133

Bradington-Young, 86, 94
Breakfront, 96
Broyhill, 47, 102, 113
Buffet, 118
Bureau, 50
Burl, 24, 28, 31
Bushings, nylon, 21

C

Cabinetmaking, 7
Calia, 86
Carving, 3, 10, 24-25, 29-30, 53
Casegoods, xi, 11, 27, 102, 104
Catnapper, 94
Cedar, 30, 33
Century Furniture, 7, 102, 117-118
Chairs, xi, 1, 3, 7, 21, 36, 54, 56, 57, 58, 63, 66, 71, 74, 75, 81, 96, 109, 123, 128
Chateau d'Ax, 86
Cherry, 25, 29-30, 97, 119, 126-127
Chest, xi, 2, 27, 28, 50, 53, 61

China cabinet, xi, 18, 23, 25, 54, 56
Chipcore, 24
Chippendale, 3, 8, 96
Cleaning:
    leather, 90
    upholstery, 78-79
    wood, 36-37
Collection, of furniture, x, xi, 4, 9, 29, 61
Comparison pricing, 44
Comparison shopping, 43
Computer desk, 4, 59
Consignment, 41, 45-46
Core, of cushions, 71-72, 87
Cotton, 75-76, 81-85
Country style, 6-7, 10, 29, 45, 54, 86, 89, 96-97, 102-105, 108-110, 113-114, 116, 118, 120, 124, 126, 128, 131, 133
Crawford, Ilse, 96, 133
Curio cabinet, xi
Cushions, xi, 47, 63, 66, 67, 71, 72, 78, 8789

D

Dacron, 63, 67, 71-72, 76, 84
Damask, 81-82
Deck:
      eight-way hand-tied, xi, 67, 69
      of sofa, xi, 64
      self, 64
Deluxing, 60
Design elements, 6, 8, 23
Desk, 4, 59, 102
Directoire, 4
Discounters, 106, 121-122
Display cabinets, 18
Doors, 18, 21, 23, 39, 49, 59
Dowel, 66
Down, for cushions, 63, 71-72, 76
Drawer guides, 21
Drawers, 11, 18, 21, 23, 26-27, 50
Dresser, xi, 23, 27, 49, 50, 53, 61
Drexel-Heritage, xi, 7, 23, 41, 46, 77, 102, 103, 104, 106, 118
Dust panel, 21
Dye:
      aniline, 35, 87-88, 90-92
      for fabric, 80, 82-83
      for leather, 87-88, 90-92

E

E.J. Victor, 77, 104
Eclectic, 9, 96
Egypt, 1, 33
Elm, 30, 65
Embroidery, 81, 83
Empire period, 4
English influence, 4, 6, 10, 28-29, 31, 82, 96
Entertainment center, 4, 58-59
Ethan Allen, 41, 45, 77, 102-103, 105, 127-128

F

Family room, 56-60, 88, 118
Feathers, 63
Fiber, for textiles, 75-77, 83-84, 90
Fiberboard, 21

Fiberglass, 82
Finish:
      abuse of, 36-37
      chemicals on, 36-37
      conversion, 35
      cost, 13, 25-26
      crazing, 24
      deep, xi, 21, 34, 35
      fabric, 80-85
      film, 35
      first aid for, 37-39
      heat on, 25, 33, 37, 58, 82
      leather, 25, 91-92
      nitro-cellulose lacquer, 35
      penetrating, 35
      photoengraved, 13, 21
      plastic laminates, 35, 61
      protection of, 34-35, 37, 56
      protective, 35, 81, 92
      runs, 25
      steps, 27, 35
      sunlight on, 33, 36-37, 60-61
      system, 35
      thickness , 35
      for wood, 11, 13, 21, 23, 27, 32, 34-35, 37, 57
Flexner, Bob, 36-37, 133
Flexsteel, 102
Frame, 65
      chamfered, 63
      components, 65, 89
      contoured, 64, 66
      hardwood, 64
      of leather item, 87-89
      padding of, 66-67
      for upholstery, 62-67, 69, 79
French:
      Burl, 31
      influence, 3-4, 6, 10, 50, 80, 84, 96, 131
      polishing, 35
Frisé, 74, 82

G

Georgian style, 4
Glides, for legs, 21, 23
Glue, 13, 26, 34, 37, 66
Glue blocks, 26
Goddard, 4
Gopher wood, 33
Great Bed of Ware, 50

Gum lac, 34-35
Guy-Chaddock, 104

H

Hackberry, 65
Hancock & Moore, 86, 94, 102
Hand:
      defined
         of fabric, 75-76, 83-84
         of leather, 87, 92
Hand work, 7, 13, 82-84
Harden Furniture, 104
Hardware, 21, 27, 38, 90, 97, 106
Headboard, xi, 49, 53, 126
Hekman Furniture, 102
Henredon, 7, 46, 77, 86, 102, 104, 115, 117-118
Hepplewhite style, 3, 8
Heritage, 77
High boy, 53
Highland House, 77, 102
Hinckle Harris, 104
Hooker Furniture, 103
Hutch, 2

I

Interior Designer, 94, 111
Interline, 86
Ital Design, 86
Italian influence, 3, 87-89

J

Jacobean style, 4, 81

K

Karges Furniture, 104, 118
Kindel Furniture, 104
Klaussner, 86, 89

L

La-Z-Boy, 41, 86, 94, 105, 113, 119, 127
Lane Furniture, 78, 103
Leather Center, 86
Leather Trend, 86
Leather, Italian, 86, 88
Legs, 1, 11, 21, 23-25, 56, 64-66
Leveling devices, 18, 56

Lexington, 103, 117
Lighting, 18, 58, 97, 111-112
Linen, 75, 81, 83, 85
Linen-fold carving, 2
Lingerie chest. *See* semainier
Louis of France, 3-4, 7, 10

M

Magazines, 93, 96-97, 120,
  123, 130-133
Mahogany, xi, 3, 7, 25, 27, 28,
  29, 30, 31, 66
  African, 31
  Honduras, 31
  imitating, 30
  Philippine, 31
  white, 32
Maintenance. *See* cleaning
Maitland-Smith, 103
Manufacturers
  list of, 101-105
  ranking of, 77
Manufacturing flow chart, 11
Maple, x, 29-32, 65
Marge Carson, 104
Margin, 41-43
Markup, 42
Marshall unit, 63
Matelasse, 82
Mattress, 47, 49-50, 106-108,
  126
Mirrors, xi, 3, 53
MSRP, 42, 44
Muslin, 71-72, 83

N

Napoleon, 1, 4-5, 34
Natuzzi, 86, 90, 103
Naugahyde. *See* vinyl
Nicoletti, 86
Night stands, xi, 53, 61, 96
Norwalk, 41, 107
Nylon fabric, 74, 76, 82-84

O

Oak, 2-3, 25, 27-32
Occasional furniture, xi, 102-
  104
Oil, olive, 38
Olefin, 76. *See also*
  polypropylene
Olive wood, 31

P

Padding, of frames. *See* Frame,
  padding of
Palliser, 86, 90
Patina, 34, 92
Pecan, 32
Pennsylvania House, 103
Philippine furniture, x, 103
Phyfe, Duncan, 4
Plush, 83
Polishing, 35
Polyester, 71, 76, 83
Polyfoam, 63, 71
Polypropylene, 66, 69, 76
Polyurethane, 71
Posts, 58
  bed, 53
Pulaski, 103
PVC, 77

Q

Queen Anne style, 3, 8
Quilting, 83

R

Racking (twisting), 65
Rail:
  of case goods, 23
  of seating, 56, 64-65
Randolph, 4, 106
Rayon, 76, 81-84
Recliners, 6, 93-94, 124, 127
Redwood, 32
Renaissance, 2, 4
Resale, 45-46
Retro, 96-97
Roman, 2-3, 8
Rosewood, 3, 32

S

Sash locks, 18
Sateen, 64, 84
Satinwood, 3, 32
Savery, 4
Saxon, 2
Seating, 57-58, 63, 100, 126
Secondhand, 46
Semainier, 50
Service, viii, 42, 44, 113, 114,
  115, 116, 117, 127
Serving carts, 56
Shaker style, 6

Shear, of fabric, 85
Shellac, 35
Sheraton, 3, 8
Sherrill, 77, 133
Sideboard, 54
Silk, 31, 75-77, 80-85, 124
Simmons, 78
Slip seats, 56
Sofa, xi, 43, 44, 45, 57, 59,
  63, 64, 65, 66, 67, 69, 70,
  71, 72, 74, 75, 79, 80, 83,
  84, 85, 86, 87, 8889-91, 93-
  94, 98-100, 106, 109-111,
  113, 123, 126-128
Soft Line, 86
Springs, 63, 66-67, 69, 71, 89,
  131
Stanley Furniture, 103
Stewart, Martha, 10, 96, 128
Stickley Furniture, 104, 115
Stiles, 23
Stoddard, Alexandra, 96, 133
Stores, 105-108
Strato-Lounger, 94
Stretchers (for chair legs), 56
Suite, xi
Sumter Cabinet, 103
Synthetics. *See* fiber, for
  textiles

T

Tables, x, xi, 1, 2, 3, 7, 11, 21,
  23, 35, 36, 37, 46, 54, 56,
  58, 78, 109
  accessory, xi
  cocktail, xi, 23, 46, 58
  dining, 23, 29, 38, 47, 54,
  56, 60, 128
  end, xi, 78
  glass, 23, 54, 124
  leaves of, 11, 18, 23, 26, 54,
  56
  pads for, 56
  pedestal, 54
  slide mechanism, 54
  tops of, 38, 54, 56, 124
Tapestry, 80, 84
Teak, 32, 35
Thomasville, 7, 41, 46, 77, 86,
  102-103, 105, 113, 118
Triacetate, 76
Tudor style, 3
Tulip wood, 3

Turnbuckle, 23
Turpentine, 34
Tweed, 84

U

Universal Furniture, 103
Used furniture, 41

V

Varnish, 29, 34
Vaughan-Bassett, 104
Velvet, 83-85, 87
Veneer:
  art of, 13
  benefits of, 13
  book about, 133
  construction, 13, 26
  definition of, 27

foundation for, 24
history of, 1, 10
match, 26
thickness , 27
wood for, 26
Victorian, 4, 8, 53, 132
Vinyl, 77, 85, 89, 91, 125-126

W

Walnut, 3, 27-30, 32, 35
  black, 30
  grafted, 31
  Persian (French Burl), 31
  white (butternut), 30
Wardrobe, 53
Warehouse sale, 43-44
Warp, of fabric, 80, 84
Warranty, 60, 79-80, 88
Watertown slides, 23, 54, 56

Wax:
  for batik, 80
  beeswax, 34
  candle, 38
  drawer guide lubrication, 21
  paste, 37-38
  for polishing wood, 36-37
  stick, 38
Wood:
  construction with, 13, 30
  kiln-dried, 8, 26, 63, 65, 126
  stability, 13, 21, 26, 54, 64
  warping of, 29, 65
Wool, 75-76, 81-84

NOTES

NOTES

NOTES

NOTES

_____

_____

_____

_____

_____

_____

_____

_____

_____

_____

_____

_____

_____

_____

_____

_____

_____

_____

NOTES

NOTES

_____

_____

_____

_____

_____

_____

_____

_____

_____

_____

_____

_____

_____

_____

_____

_____

_____

NOTES

NOTES